T0311448

Cambridge Elements ≡

Elements in Construction Grammar
edited by
Thomas Hoffmann
Catholic University of Eichstätt-Ingolstadt
Alexander Bergs
Osnabrück University

THE CONSTRUCTICON

Taxonomies and Networks

Holger Diessel
Friedrich Schiller University Jena

CAMBRIDGE
UNIVERSITY PRESS

Shaftesbury Road, Cambridge CB2 8EA, United Kingdom

One Liberty Plaza, 20th Floor, New York, NY 10006, USA

477 Williamstown Road, Port Melbourne, VIC 3207, Australia

314–321, 3rd Floor, Plot 3, Splendor Forum, Jasola District Centre, New Delhi – 110025, India

103 Penang Road, #05–06/07, Visioncrest Commercial, Singapore 238467

Cambridge University Press is part of Cambridge University Press & Assessment, a department of the University of Cambridge.

We share the University's mission to contribute to society through the pursuit of education, learning and research at the highest international levels of excellence.

www.cambridge.org
Information on this title: www.cambridge.org/9781009327817

DOI: 10.1017/9781009327848

First published 2023

A catalogue record for this publication is available from the British Library.

ISBN 978-1-009-32781-7 Paperback
ISSN 2753-2674 (online)
ISSN 2753-2666 (print)

The Constructicon

Taxonomies and Networks

Elements in Construction Grammar

DOI: 10.1017/9781009327848
First published online: May 2023

Holger Diessel
Friedrich Schiller University Jena

Author for correspondence: Holger Diessel, holger.diessel@uni-jena.de

Abstract: It is one of the central claims of construction grammar that constructions are organized in some kind of network, commonly referred to as the constructicon. In the classical model of construction grammar, developed by Berkeley linguists in the 1990s, the constructicon is an inheritance network of taxonomically related grammatical patterns. However, recent research in usage-based linguistics has expanded the classical inheritance model into a multidimensional network approach in which constructions are interrelated by multiple types of associations. The multidimensional network approach challenges long-standing assumptions of linguistic research and calls for a reorganization of the constructivist approach. This Element describes how the conception of the constructicon has changed in recent years and elaborates on some central claims of the multidimensional network approach.

Keywords: construction grammar, constructicon, grammar network, usage-based, cognitive linguistics

ISBNs: 9781009327817 (PB), 9781009327848 (OC)
ISSNs: 2753-2674 (online), 2753-2666 (print)

Contents

1 Introduction

Construction grammar makes two central claims (Hoffmann and Trousdale 2013). The first claim is that linguistic structure consists of conventional pairings of form and meaning, that is, constructions. The second claim is that constructions are integrated into a system, known as the **constructicon** (sometimes written **construct-i-con**; Jurafsky 1991). There is a large body of research on the structure, meaning, acquisition, and change of particular constructions (for reviews, see Hilpert 2014; Hoffmann 2022); but there is relatively little research on the constructicon. As Lyngfelt (2018: 1) noted in a recent paper, although researchers agree that constructions are integrated into a system, "the internal structure of the constructicon is still largely uncharted territory."

In the classical model of construction grammar, the constructicon is an inheritance hierarchy or taxonomy (Fillmore and Kay 1999). Inheritance is a key concept of formal varieties of construction grammar (Fillmore and Kay 1999; Sag 2012) but has also been used by Goldberg (1995) and other cognitive linguists to describe the cognitive organization of grammar. Following the pioneering work of Goldberg, it has become a standard assumption of cognitive linguistics that the constructicon is mainly a taxonomy in which lower-level constructions inherit general properties from higher-level constructions. The inheritance model of the constructicon has dominated research in construction grammar for more than two decades, but recent research in usage-based linguistics argues that, while grammar includes an important taxonomic dimension, constructions are not only taxonomically related. Combining evidence from linguistics with insights from psychology, these studies argue that a person's knowledge of grammar involves multiple types of associations that characterize the constructicon as a multidimensional network (e.g. Kapatsinski 2018; Lyngfeld et al. 2018; Diessel 2019a; Schmid 2020; Sommerer and Smirnova 2020).

The multidimensional network approach presents a radical alternative to the structuralist and generative traditions of linguistic research but also poses new challenges to the constructivist approach. While the classical inheritance model has abandoned key concepts of structuralist and generative linguistics (e.g. the distinction between lexicon and grammar), it has maintained the traditional conception of many syntactic phenomena. The multidimensional network approach takes construction grammar to a whole new level. As we will see, if we think of grammar as an association network shaped by language use, we need new formats of linguistic representation for all linguistic concepts, including the key concept of construction grammar, that is, the notion of construction.

In what follows, I first describe the development of the constructicon from the classical inheritance model to the multidimensional network approach (Section 2) and then expand on three central claims of current research in usage-based construction grammar: (i) the definition of constructions as dynamic networks (Section 3), (ii) the emergence of syntactic categories from different types of associations (Section 4), and (iii) the global organization of the constructicon into paradigms, families, and neighborhoods (Section 5).

2 From Taxonomies to Networks

The classical model of construction grammar was developed by a group of Berkeley linguists in the late 1980s and 1990s. From the very beginning, there were two main varieties of construction grammar: a formal variety, developed by Fillmore and Kay (1999), which was primarily concerned with the development of a formal system for representing constructions, and a cognitive variety, developed by Lakoff (1987) and Goldberg (1995), which was primarily concerned with cognitive aspects of constructions (cf. Boas 2013). Although the two varieties had different goals, they strongly influenced each other during the early stages of construction grammar, with far-reaching consequences for the conception of the constructicon. This Element concentrates on cognitive varieties of construction grammar, which later developed into usage-based construction grammar.[1]

2.1 The Grammar–Lexicon Continuum

It is one of the central claims of traditional linguistic theory that linguistic knowledge comprises two basic components: (i) a lexicon including words and idioms and (ii) grammar including syntactic categories and rules. Construction grammar has challenged this view, arguing that, if we think of linguistic structure in terms of constructions, lexicon and grammar form a continuum rather than two separate components. The reconceptualization of lexicon and grammar as a continuum laid the foundation for the initial conception of the

---

[1] Formal varieties of construction grammar will not be considered in this Element. Note, however, that some recent computational approaches to construction grammar have extended the formal inheritance model to a multidimensional network approach that shares important properties with the usage-based view of the constructicon (e.g. Steels 2011; van Trijp 2016; Boas 2017; Lyngfelt et al. 2018). It is a task of future research to integrate theoretical and computational research on the constructicon into a unified approach.

constructicon in which words, idioms, and all grammatical patterns are analyzed as constructions.

The notion of construction has a long history in linguistics that predates the rise of construction grammar. Traditionally, the term "construction" refers to particular clause or sentence types, such as the passive or questions, that are analyzed by **construction-particular rules**, that is, rules that are exclusively needed to explain a particular structural pattern or construction. Active declarative main clauses are traditionally excluded from constructional analysis as they do not seem to involve construction-particular rules. To illustrate, a passive sentence, such as *He was invited by John*, has idiosyncratic properties that can be explained by construction-particular rules: A passive sentence encodes the patient as grammatical subject, includes a special verb form that does not appear in any other sentence type, and may express the agent in a *by*-phrase. In contrast to the passive, active declarative main clauses are usually seen as fully regular grammatical patterns that do not involve construction-particular rules. An active sentence, such as *She opens the door*, for example, instantiates the SVO word order pattern that also appears in many other clause and sentence types, accords with general phrase structure rules, and is semantically predictable from its lexical components.

In the classical version of generative grammar, constructions, such as the passive and questions, were derived from underlying representations of active declarative main clauses by syntactic transformations (Chomsky 1965). Later versions of generative grammar abandoned syntactic transformations and analyzed all syntactic structures, including those that are traditionally regarded as constructions, by the same set of syntactic categories and structure-building operations such as "merge" and "move." As Chomsky (1995: 4) put it in *The Minimalist Program*: "The notion of grammatical construction is eliminated, and with it, construction-particular rules."

Construction grammar has taken the opposite route and has extended the notion of construction from the analysis of particular clause and sentence types to all syntactic patterns including basic declarative main clauses. There were several reasons for this (for discussion, see Hilpert 2014; Hoffmann 2022), but of particular importance was that researchers began to recognize that natural language abounds with idiomatic and formulaic sequences. In an important paper, Fillmore et al. (1988) showed that idiomaticity is a matter of degree that concerns all clause and sentence types (Nunberg et al. 1994). Since there is no clear division between regular and idiomatic forms, these researchers argued that syntactic structure is best analyzed by a general notion of construction that applies to all clause and sentence types including basic declarative main clauses.

Table 1 Examples of different types of constructions
(cf. Goldberg 2006: 5)

Construction type	Examples
Morpheme	*un-, -ize, -ed*
Word	*banana, return, but*
Complex word	*motorway, armchair*
Complex word (partially filled)	[V-*ize*], [N-*ment*]
Idiom (filled)	*kick the bucket, pull a fast one*
Comparative correlative	*the* Xer *the* Yer
Resultative construction	SUBJ V OBJ A/PP$_{result}$
Passive construction	SUBJ aux VPPTC (PP*by*)

Abandoning the categorical distinction between regular and idiomatic expressions, Fillmore and colleagues defined constructions as **signs**, or symbols, that combine a particular form with meaning, similar to words or lexemes. A transitive sentence, for example, can be seen as a complex linguistic sign that maps a particular structural pattern (i.e. SVO) onto a particular semantic representation of a transitive event. Assuming that syntactic structure consists of signs, many construction grammarians use the notion of construction not only for syntactic patterns but also for lexical expressions and even for bound morphemes (Table 1).[2] On this view, a person's knowledge of language consists of nothing but constructions (Hilpert 2014: 2), or as Goldberg (2003: 223) put it in an oft-cited phrase: "it's constructions all the way down."

If language consists of nothing but constructions, it is just consequent to abandon the traditional distinction between lexicon and grammar in favor of a more uniform approach in which all linguistic signs, for example morphemes, words, phrases, and clause-level constructions, are represented within the same system that has become known as the constructicon. But how is this system organized? What is the structure of the constructicon?

2.2 Inheritance Networks

2.2.1 The Classical Inheritance Model

In the classical model of construction grammar, the constructicon is an inheritance hierarchy or taxonomy (Goldberg 1995: 67). The term **inheritance** was borrowed from computer science, notably from object-oriented programing,

---

[2] The status of morphemes as constructions is a matter of debate (for discussion, see Ungerer and Hartmann 2023).

where it describes a mechanism whereby lower-level (child) objects inherit general information from higher-level (parent) objects (Shieber 2003). The linguistic use of the term "inheritance" is related to its use in computer science. In particular, formal varieties of construction grammar use the notion of inheritance in a way similar to that in computer science (Fillmore and Kay 1999; Sag 2012). The general idea behind linguistic inheritance is simple. Linguistic generalizations are represented in schematic parent constructions from which lower-level child constructions inherit shared features. For example, English has many different types of relative clauses that vary with regard to a wide range of features, for example word order, verb form, and the syntactic function of the nominal head in the relative clause (1a–d).

(1) a. The man [who talked to me] ...   finite, subject
     b. The man [(who) I talked to] ...   finite, nonsubject
     c. The picture [showing John] ...   nonfinite, present participle
     d. The picture [shown to John] ...   nonfinite, past participle

What (almost) all relative clauses have in common is that they modify a noun or noun phrase of the main clause that serves a syntactic function (and semantic role) inside of the relative clause. Relative clauses can, thus, be represented in a taxonomy in which specific types of relative clauses inherit shared features from more abstract representations (2).

(2)

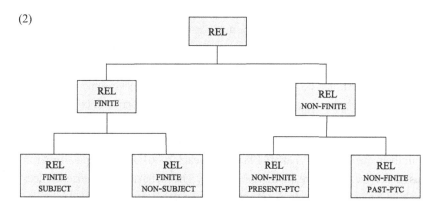

Formal construction grammar uses feature matrices to explain how constructions of different degrees of specificity are connected by inheritance relations (Fillmore and Kay 1999; Sag 2012). Cognitive construction grammar makes little use of feature matrices but adopts the general notion of inheritance to explain how linguistic generalizations are represented in the constructicon. There is abundant evidence from psycholinguistics that knowledge of grammar includes both local and global generalizations (Bates and MacWhinney 1989), which cognitive linguists represent by constructions at different levels of abstraction that are connected by inheritance relations (Goldberg 1995). In other words, cognitive construction grammar uses the term "inheritance" as some kind of cognitive or psychological concept, which must not be confused with the notion of inheritance in computer science and formal grammar.

Nevertheless, although cognitive inheritance is not identical to the formal mechanism of inheritance, the latter had a significant impact on cognitive research on the constructicon. Both formal grammar and computer science distinguish between two different inheritance models: (i) the **impoverished entry model**, in which shared information is stored only once at the highest level of abstraction, and (ii) the **full entry model**, in which shared information is represented at multiple levels of the inheritance hierarchy. Considering the two formal inheritance models, Goldberg (1995: 74) argued that, from a cognitive perspective, the full entry model is more adequate as linguistic information about structure and meaning is often stored redundantly at different levels of abstraction (see also Langacker 1987, who refers to this as the **rule–list fallacy**).

Another distinction that Goldberg and other cognitive linguists adopted from computer science and formal grammar is the distinction between complete and default inheritance. In the **complete mode of inheritance**, child objects are fully consistent with their parents; but in the **default mode of inheritance**, there can be some minor conflict in value between child and parent objects. Fillmore and Kay (1999) used the complete mode of inheritance to build a formal model of construction grammar; but if we think of constructions as cognitive entities, the default mode of inheritance seems to be more adequate as it provides a mechanism to account for grammatical exceptions (Goldberg 1995: 73–74). "All grammars leak" (Sapir 1921: 38), that is, all grammatical generalizations have some exceptions, which is difficult to reconcile with the complete mode of inheritance but consistent with default inheritance since the default mode of inheritance allows lower-level constructions to override higher-level constructions if they are not fully consistent with their specifications (Lakoff 1987; Langacker 2000). For example, earlier in this section we said that relative clauses modify a noun, but this generalization does not hold for sentential relatives, which modify, or elaborate, a whole clause (cf. *He passed the exam, which surprised us*). Table 2 summarizes the previous discussion and provides an overview of the various types of inheritance models considered in early research on the constructicon.

2.2.2 Different Types of Inheritance Relations

In addition to standard inheritance links (sometimes called **instance links**), Goldberg (1995: 75–89) proposed three other, more specific types of inheritance

Table 2 Models of inheritance

Inheritance models	Impoverished entry model	Full entry model
	Shared information is stored only once at the highest level	Shared information is stored redundantly at multiple levels
Mode of inheritance	**Complete mode**	**Default mode**
	High- and low-level representations are fully compatible with each other	Low-level representations override high-level representations if there is a conflict

relations: (i) polysemy links, (ii) metaphorical links, and (iii) subpart links. **Polysemy links** and **metaphorical links** designate semantically motivated inheritance relations between semantic subtypes of the same construction. For example, the caused-motion construction (NP V NP PP_{LOC}) designates an act of transfer whereby an agent causes an object to move somewhere (3a–b) (Goldberg 1995: 152–179).

(3)   a. He pushed me into the car.   [X causes Y to move Z]
            b. She shoved it into the drawer.

Yet, in addition to encoding transfer, the caused-motion construction occurs with several other related meanings, which Goldberg (1995) described as extensions of its basic meaning. For example, the sentences in (4a–b) designate a scene in which an agent helps another person to move somewhere, and the sentences in (5a–b) designate a scene in which an agent enables another person to move somewhere.

(4)   a. He helped him into the car.   [X helps Y to move Z]
            b. She guided him through the terrain.

(5)   a. He allowed Bob out of the room.   [X enables Y to move Z]
            b. She let him into her office.

Considering these uses, Goldberg (1995: 161–174) argued that the caused-motion construction is polysemous. Or more generally, she maintained that argument-structure constructions, such as the caused-motion construction, are organized in semantic networks in which the various subtypes of a construction inherit general semantic properties from its basic meaning and use (6).

(6)

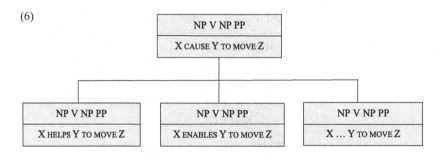

Subpart links are considered only briefly in Goldberg (1995: 78–79) and defined as follows: "A subpart link is posited when one construction is a proper subpart of another construction and exists independently." For example, transitive and intransitive argument-structure constructions are related by a subpart link, according to Goldberg, as the intransitive construction constitutes a proper subpart of a corresponding transitive construction (7).

(7)

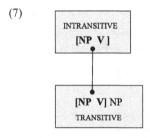

Subpart links have also been proposed in a few other studies (Croft 2001; Booij 2010; Hilpert 2014), but there is no systematic discussion of subpart links anywhere in the construction-based literature. Several studies used the term "subpart link" in conjunction with **multiple inheritance** (Hilpert 2014: 62–63), a phenomenon whereby a lower-level construction inherits properties from "multiple parents" (Croft 2001: 25). For example, Croft (2001) argued that the sentence *I didn't sleep* inherits properties from (at least) two schematic parent constructions: (i) the intransitive construction and (ii) a negative construction that is defined by the occurrence of an auxiliary, a negative marker, and the semantic feature of negation (8) (adapted from Croft 2001: 26).

(8)

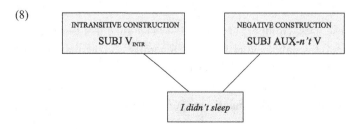

Multiple inheritance accounts have also been proposed for English relative clauses (Sag 2012), argument-structure questions (Croft 2001: 26), and syntactic amalgams (Michaelis and Lambrecht 1996; Hilpert 2014). For example, Hilpert (2014: 63–64) argued that the sentence in (9) includes a syntactic amalgam that inherits properties from two interlaced constructions: (i) the nominal attribute construction (e.g. *an important song*) and (ii) the *enough-to* infinitive construction (e.g. *is important enough to put on*).

(9)   It was **[an important] enough [song] to put on** the last single.

Polysemy links, subpart links, and multiple inheritance links are useful for analyzing particular aspects of the constructicon; but note that Goldberg (1995: 75–81) described all of these links as inheritance relations. In the classical model of construction grammar, the constructicon is a taxonomy or hierarchy of constructions that are connected by "different types of inheritance relations" (Goldberg 1995: 75).

An important extension of the taxonomic conception of the constructicon is **Radical Construction Grammar**, developed by Croft (2001). Radical Construction Grammar approaches the analysis of constructions from a cross-linguistic perspective and extends the constructivist view of linguistic structure to syntactic categories, for example word classes and syntactic functions. We will discuss the contributions of Radical Construction Grammar to the development of the constructicon in Section 4. In the remainder of the current section, we consider how the classical inheritance model of the constructicon, as devised by Goldberg (1995), has been extended into a multidimensional network approach in which constructions are related by different types of associations. The development is closely related to the rise of the usage-based model (Langacker 2000; Bybee 2006, 2010) and the quantitative turn in cognitive linguistics (Janda 2013).

2.3 The Usage-Based Model

The usage-based model has evolved from several strands of research in functional and cognitive linguistics (Hopper 1987; Langacker 2000; Bybee 2010) and related research in cognitive psychology (Bates and MacWhinney 1989; Tomasello 2003) and cognitive science (Elman et al. 1996; Steels 2015). In the structuralist and generative traditions of linguistics, grammar is a closed deductive system consisting of primitive categories and algorithmic rules similar to categories and rules in mathematics or formal logic. Challenging this view, usage-based linguists have characterized grammar as a **dynamic system** in which categories and rules, or constructions, are shaped by domain-general processes of language use. **Domain-general processes** are cognitive processes that are operative not only in language but also in other cognitive domains, for example in vison or nonlinguistic memory (Ibbotson 2020). Examples of domain-general processes include categorization, analogy, and social cognition. All of these processes have been studied independently of language in general psychological research on human cognition (Anderson 2005). Since domain-general processes are sensitive to frequency of use, usage-based linguists emphasize the importance of **usage frequency** for grammatical analysis (e.g. Bybee and Hopper 2001; Diessel 2007; Diessel and Hilpert 2016; Divjak 2019). In the usage-based approach, grammar is a probabilistic system in which categories and constructions are constantly updated, restructured, and reorganized under the influence of language use (for reviews, see Bybee and Beckner 2010; Diessel 2017).

There are various proposals to model the effect of usage on grammar. One popular approach is **stochastic grammar**, which consists of two components: (i) a formal grammar including categories and rules as in traditional phrase structure grammar and (ii) a probabilistic component that augments the elements of formal grammar by probability scores based on their frequency in a corpus (Manning and Schütze 1999). Stochastic grammars are widely used in natural language processing to resolve structural ambiguities. For example, the sentence *Paul kept the dogs on the beach* is structurally ambiguous between two interpretations: The clause-final PP can be an adjunct (attached to VP) or a noun modifier (attached to NP). Stochastic grammars weigh the two interpretations by assigning probability scores to phrase structure rules and valency patterns, as illustrated in (10a–b) adapted from Jurafsky (1996: 28).

(10)   a.

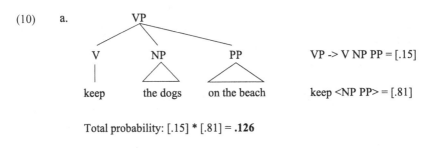

Total probability: [.15] * [.81] = **.126**

       b.

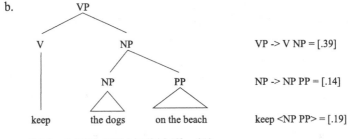

Total probability: [.39] * [.14] * [.19] = **.010**

As can be seen, the two interpretations involve different phrase structure rules. Each phrase structure rule has a probability score that indicates its probability of being chosen by a parser (or language user) based on its frequency in a large corpus. In addition, the verb *keep* is assigned two probability scores that reflect the likelihood of *keep* being used in one or the other phrase structure pattern. If we multiply the probabilities of the verb with the probabilities of the various phrase-structure rules in the two interpretations, we obtain two global probability scores that allow the parser to resolve the ambiguity by selecting the interpretation that receives a higher score. Thus, in (10) the interpretation of the clause-final PP as verbal adjunct (10a) is much more probable, and therefore more likely to be selected in language use, than the interpretation as noun modifier (10b).

Stochastic grammars are useful to model the effect of usage frequency on the storage and processing of linguistic structure, but they do not explain how these structures emerge and change. What is needed are more dynamic formats of linguistic representation that allow researchers to account for the emergence of linguistic structure and meaning. There are two important proposals in the usage-based literature to accomplish this: one that builds on exemplar theory and another one that is inspired by network science. The two approaches are not mutually exclusive and are often combined in usage-based studies (Bybee 2006; Goldberg 2006). Yet, for expository purposes, we will keep them separate.

2.3.1 The Exemplar Approach

Exemplar theory is a psychological theory of categorization (Nosofsky 1988) that has been especially prominent in usage-based research on phonetics and morphology (Bybee 1985, 2001; Pierrehumbert 2003). In this approach, categories are formed from similar experiences that are grouped together into clusters of similar memory traces. New experiences are categorized based on their similarity to stored exemplars, or clusters of stored memory traces. Exemplar theory provides a straightforward account for the effect of frequency on memory and categorization: Every experience leaves a trace in memory; similar experiences reinforce each other and function as analogical attractors for the classification of novel experiences.

Exemplar theory has been used to account for the emergence and classification of phonetic categories (Bybee 2001; Pierrehumbert 2003). For example, young infants can initially discriminate all kinds of speech sounds, including speech sounds that are not conventional in the ambient language. However, after a few months they become particularly sensitive to the speech sounds of their own language and lose the ability to discriminate speech sounds of other languages (for a review of relevant research, see Werker et al. 2012). In a series of experiments, Maye et al. (2002) showed that infants' changing capacity of discriminating speech sounds across languages is crucially determined by the frequency and similarity of speech sounds infants encounter in the input, which Pierrehumbert (2003) and others interpreted as evidence for exemplar learning in phonological development.

Bybee (1995, 2001) extended the exemplar approach from phonetics and phonology to morphology. Like speech sounds, words and morphemes can be seen as exemplar categories. As Bybee (2010) put it:

> [E]ach of the phonetic forms of a word that are distinguishable are established in memory as exemplars; new tokens of experience that are the same as some existing exemplars are mapped on to it, strengthening it. Then all the phonetic exemplars are grouped together in an exemplar cluster which is associated with the meanings of the word and the contexts in which it has been used, which themselves form an exemplar cluster. (Bybee 2010: 19)

Assuming that syntactic structure consists of linguistic signs, that is, constructions, it is a small step from words (or morphology) to phrases and sentences (or syntax). Like speech sounds and lexemes, syntactic constructions have been analyzed as exemplar categories. If the same construction is repeatedly used with some minor variation, it becomes entrenched in memory as a cluster of overlapping exemplars that influence the categorization of the same or similar instances of that construction in future use (Bybee 2006). The exemplar view of constructions has been very prominent for the past fifteen years and is immanent in Goldberg's most recent definition of the term "construction":

> [C]onstructions are understood to be emergent clusters of lossy memory traces that are aligned within our high- (hyper-!) dimensional conceptual space on the basis of shared form, function, and contextual dimensions. (Goldberg 2019: 7)

Exemplar theory provides a dynamic framework for analyzing the emergence of linguistic structure and meaning. It does away with primitive concepts and explains how linguistic structures are shaped by usage and why they never really reach a stable state as a person's linguistic knowledge is constantly updated by novel experiences.

Nevertheless, while exemplar theory is useful to explain some aspects of language emergence, recent studies argue that the exemplar view of language is not fully adequate for modeling grammar. The main point of critique concerns the representation of abstract linguistic knowledge. In a pure exemplar model, there are no abstract representations that are permanently stored in memory (Nosofsky 1988). As Bybee and Beckner (2010) put it with reference to constructions:

> [I]n an exemplar model, constructions are not abstract grammatical patterns but rather they are sets of experienced exemplars arranged in cognitive space to reflect their similarity in form and meaning. (Bybee and Beckner 2010: 843)

Having said this, Bybee and Beckner make it clear that a person's knowledge of constructions also includes schematic representations of linguistic structure and meaning. Usage-based linguists have emphasized the importance of stored experiences for grammatical analysis (Bybee 2006, 2007), but there is widespread consensus among cognitive and usage-based linguists that grammar also includes schemas of form and meaning that are not captured by a pure exemplar model (Abbott-Smith and Tomasello 2006; Goldberg 2006). This has led researchers to combine exemplar theory with other models of categorization that include abstract representations or schemas. A **schema** is a conceptual template with holistic properties that can combine a particular structure with meaning (as in the case of schematic constructions), but a schema can also represent a purely formal or purely semantic pattern.

The absence of schematic representations is only one reason why a pure exemplar model does not seem to be appropriate for analyzing a person's linguistic knowledge (for discussion, see Diessel 2016). Language is a highly complex system that includes many different types of concepts (e.g. lexemes, syntactic categories, and schematic constructions) that interact with each other in intricate ways and that cannot simply be explained by clusters of overlapping tokens. In order to account for the emergence of schemas and the interaction of linguistic categories, we need a more structured approach that differentiates between different types of linguistic knowledge (e.g. schematic vs. concrete) and different types of categories (e.g. constructions, word classes, syntactic functions). In accordance with this view, several recent studies have expanded the traditional inheritance model of construction grammar into a multidimensional network approach.

2.3.2 The Multidimensional Network Approach

The multidimensional network approach is inspired by network science (in a broad sense of the term; e.g. Elman et al. 1996; Buchanan 2002). Network models are used in many scientific disciplines to analyze a wide range of phenomena, for example the economy, the climate, the brain. There are many different types of network models, but most are used to analyze dynamic and self-organizing processes, that is, processes whereby global phenomena emerge (unintentionally) from many interacting parts. Since usage-based linguists conceive of language as an emergent and self-organizing system, network models are well-suited for analyzing grammar in the usage-based approach.

Another motivation for analyzing language as a network is, of course, that the human brain and mind are commonly described as networks (Elman et al. 1996; Sporns 2012). As it stands, the network models of usage-based construction grammar are a far cry from the network models neuroscientists use to analyze the brain; but modeling linguistic and neurological processes within the same general framework (i.e. network science) may help to narrow the gap between these disciplines. Similar remarks apply to the relationship between linguistics and psychology. In cognitive psychology, memory is commonly described as an association network (Anderson 2005: 183–190). In accordance with this view, the mental lexicon is often analyzed as a network of related lexical concepts (Dell 1986; Aitchison 2012). There are also associative network accounts of morphology (Bybee 2007) and syntax (Hudson 2007); but, while usage-based linguists agree that grammar constitutes some kind of network, it is only recently that they have begun to systematically analyze the constructicon as an association network (Bybee 2010; Kapatsinski 2018; Diessel 2019a; Schmid 2020).

The classical inheritance model of construction grammar is not an association network. As we have seen, construction grammar adopted the notion of inheritance from computer science where it describes a formal mechanism for combining child and parent objects. Cognitive construction grammar has linked the notion of inheritance to psychological concepts such as categorization and abstraction; but, even in cognitive construction grammar, inheritance relations are not usually described as associations. Associations are cognitive links of human memory that have little in common with the inheritance links of classical construction grammar. Here are some of the properties that characterize associations in cognitive psychology (for a review of psychological research on associations, see Bower 2000):

- Associations originate from specific experiences.
- They are strengthened by frequency of use.
- They are sensitive to recency effects or priming.
- They are often motivated by the perception of similarity and contrast.
- They are influenced by the observer's interest.
- They are influenced by competing links and neighboring concepts.

Many of these properties have played no role in the classical inheritance model of construction grammar but are essential to the multidimensional network approach. The inheritance model of cognitive construction grammar is a hybrid model that combines aspects of cognitive psychology with aspects of formal grammar, whereas the multidimensional network approach (of usage-based linguistics) is solely motivated by psychological considerations. In this approach, the links of the constructicon are defined as specific types of associations shaped by particular domain-general processes.

In what follows, we will consider recent proposals to analyze the constructicon as an association network. The discussion is organized around three general topics: (i) the notion of construction (Section 3), (ii) the emergence of syntactic categories (Section 4), and (iii) the global organization of the constructicon (Section 5).[3]

3 Constructions as Networks

In the classical inheritance model, constructions are atomic nodes of a taxonomic network. The node-based conception of constructions has been challenged in several usage-based studies in which constructions are (re-)analyzed as networks. For example, Langacker (2000) argued that symbolic units (i.e. constructions) are organized in networks linked together by three kinds of cognitive operations: (i) symbolization, (ii) categorization, and (iii) composition. Symbolization concerns the combination of form and meaning; categorization refers to the relationship between a constructional schema and lexical expressions; and composition describes the syntagmatic organization of linguistic units. Langacker makes extensive use of the network metaphor of grammar, but his analysis of constructions as networks is not very detailed.

Schmid (2020) proposed a more elaborate network account of constructions that combines the analysis of **entrenchment** (i.e. the strengthening of linguistic information through frequency of use) with the analysis of **conventionalization** (i.e. the creation of linguistic norms in speech communities). Schmid (2016: 25) explicitly rejects the conception of constructions as nodes and argues "that linguistic knowledge is available in one format only, namely, associations."

A related network account has been proposed by Diessel (2019a, 2020). Like Schmid, Diessel defines constructions by a set of associations. However, unlike Schmid, Diessel does not entirely eliminate the node-based view of constructions. Rather, Diessel proposes a **nested network model** in which constructions are analyzed as both networks and (emergent) nodes.

---

[3] Similar types of links have been proposed in recent computational research in construction grammar that builds on frame semantics and the FrameNet project (see the collection of articles in Lyngfelt et al. 2018).

There are conspicuous parallels between these accounts: All three authors characterize constructions as dynamic networks, refer to domain-general processes in order to explain how constructions are shaped by usage, and emphasize that frequency of use has a significant impact on the representation and development of constructions. Related ideas have been expressed in several other usage-based studies (Bybee 2010; Traugott and Trousdale 2013; Lasch and Ziem 2014; Kapatsinski 2018; Goldberg 2019; Sommerer and Smirnova 2020; Hilpert 2021; Willich 2022), indicating a general trend in redefining constructions as networks.

In what follows, we will consider five different types of associations to illustrate the network approach to constructions. Each association has particular properties that are shaped by specific domain-general processes (Diessel 2020):

- **Taxonomic relations** connect constructional schemas with lexical constructions or schemas at higher or lower levels of abstraction.
- **Sequential relations**, also known as syntagmatic relations, connect symbolic units, for example words or phrases, that are frequently used together in sequential order.
- **Symbolic relations** connect a particular linguistic form, for example a word form or structural pattern, with a particular function or meaning.
- **Filler-slot relations** specify associations between the slots of constructional schemas and particular lexical or phrasal fillers.
- And **horizontal relations**, also known as lateral or sister relations, connect constructions at the same level of abstraction.

3.1 Taxonomic Relations

Taxonomic relations bear some resemblance to the inheritance links of classical construction grammar, but taxonomic and inheritance relations are not the same entities. For one, classical inheritance links are not meant to represent associations but are mainly used as a tool of formal grammar. In cognitive construction grammar, inheritance is interpreted as some kind of cognitive mechanism (Goldberg 1995); but even in cognitive construction grammar, inheritance links are not usually defined as associations. Moreover, classical inheritance links are unidirectional in the sense that they transmit information from high-level schemas to low-level constructions, but there is no upwards direction of inheritance. As Hilpert (2014: 58–59) explains: "Inheritance is [thus] a 'downwards' relation; more specific constructional characteristics are not projected 'upwards'." Taxonomic links, by contrast, are bidirectional relations that can be studied from two different perspectives (Diessel 2019a: 43–62). On the one hand, one can study how taxonomic links are created by extracting a constructional schema from lexical sequences with similar forms and meanings; and on the other hand, one can study how an existing schema is used to produce and process novel utterances, or novel instances of that schema. The bidirectional nature of taxonomic relations reflects the influence of different cognitive processes: The upwards direction is the result of abstraction (Anderson 2005: 165–167) or schematization (Langacker 2008: 17), and the downwards direction is motivated by categorization (Langacker 2000: 13) (11).

(11)

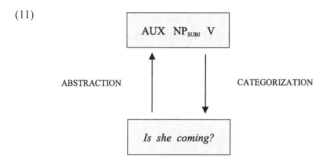

Taxonomic links are key to the usage-based study of linguistic generalizations. In formal grammar, linguistic generalizations are detached from lexical representations. Parsimony and non-redundancy are leading principles of formal grammar that ban lexical representations from the domain of grammar; but usage-based linguists take a different view. If we look at grammar from a psychological perspective, there is good evidence that information about grammatical patterns is often stored redundantly at different levels of abstraction (Bates and MacWhinney 1989; Langacker 1991). On this view, grammar includes both constructional schemas (of different degrees of specificity) and a large inventory of lexical prefabs that are connected to constructional schemas by taxonomic relations.

The extraction of constructional schemas from lexical sequences is one of the central topics of usage-based research on language acquisition (Tomasello 2003; Dąbrowska and Lieven 2005; Goldberg 2006; Behrens 2009; Diessel 2013). A central finding of this research is that children climb the abstraction ladder in a slow and piecemeal manner. The earliest multiword utterances children produce are fixed lexical strings that do not allow for any variation (e.g. *Get-it, All-gone, What-s-that?*). Shortly thereafter children begin to use **pivot schemas** consisting of a relational term, for example a verb or quantifier, and a slot that can be filled by particular types of lexical expressions (12) (adapted from Braine 1976).

(12)

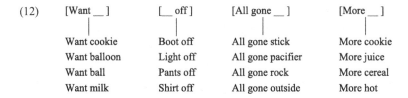

[Want __]	[__ off]	[All gone __]	[More __]
Want cookie	Boot off	All gone stick	More cookie
Want balloon	Light off	All gone pacifier	More juice
Want ball	Pants off	All gone rock	More cereal
Want milk	Shirt off	All gone outside	More hot

It takes several months, or even years, before children extract fully sche-matic constructions from pivot schemas (Tomasello 2003). One piece of evidence for the emergence of fully schematic argument-structure construc-tions comes from the occurrence of overgeneralization errors, such as those in (13a–c), that were produced by a two-to-three-year-old girl who used several intransitive verbs in the transitive schema. Since the girl is unlikely to have heard *fall*, *cough*, and *giggle* in a transitive clause, it seems reason-able to assume that she extended the early pivot use of transitive verbs (e.g. *want* __, *see* __) to a fully schematic argument-structure construction in which particular pivot verbs are replaced by a schematic V-slot for (transitive) verbs (for a review, see Diessel 2013).

(13)   a. Kendall fall that toy. [2;3]
         b. They just coughed me. [2;8]
         c. Don't giggle me. [3;0]

Children extract constructional schemas from grammatical patterns that are implicit in the lexical strings they encounter in the ambient language. But where do the implicit patterns of adult language come from? We can only speculate how constructional schemas emerged in language evolution (for some interesting sug-gestions, see Hartmann and Pleyer 2020); but we can study how constructional schemas arise in language change (Krug 2000; Van de Velde 2010; Traugott and Trousdale 2013; Hilpert 2013, 2021; Sommerer 2018; Hoffmann 2019).

    Traugott and Trousdale (2013) distinguish between two different types of grammatical change: (i) **constructional change**, which refers to the extension and modification of an existing construction or schema, and (ii) **constructio-nalization**, which refers to the emergence of an entirely new schema (or new node) in the constructicon. It seems that most grammatical change involves the extension and modification of existing constructions. Yet Traugott and Trousdale also discuss some illuminating examples of constructionalization. Similar to the emergence of constructions in L1 acquisition, novel diachronic constructions arise from the analysis of lexical sequences with similar forms and meanings. A particularly interesting case is the recent emergence of a novel VP-schema for secondary modal verbs that has evolved from a group of main verbs with modal meanings (14a–k) (Krug 2000).

(14)   Source constructions   Target constructions

    a. want to V_{INF} →   wanna /'wɒnə/ V_{INF}

    b. have to V_{INF} →   hafta /'hæftə/ V_{INF}

    c. have got to V_{INF} →   gotta /'gɒtə/ V_{INF}

    d. be going to V_{INF} →   gonna /'gɒnə/ V_{INF}

    f. need to V_{INF} →   need to /'niːtə/ V_{INF}

    g. ought to V_{INF} →   ought to /'ɔːtə/ V_{INF}

    h. try to V_{INF} →   try to /'traɪtə/ V_{INF}

    j. had better V_{INF} →   had better /'bɛtər/ V_{INF}

    k. be supposed to V_{INF} →   supposed to /'səpɔztə/ V_{INF}

The source constructions are similar but not identical. All of the verbs in (14a–k) are accompanied by a *to*-infinitive and most of them are transitive, but there is also an intransitive verb (*go*) and a verb in passive voice (*supposed*) and some verbs occur with an auxiliary or the progressive marker *-ing* (*is going to, is supposed to*). The source constructions do not form a homogeneous class; but interestingly all structural differences between them have disappeared in the course of their development into secondary modals. As Krug (2000) showed, all secondary modal verbs of Present Day English occur in the same periphrastic VP-construction in which the differences in transitivity, voice, tense, and aspect have vanished. What is more, the rise of the new modal verb schema also affected the phonetic form of the construction. As Krug (2000) observed, in colloquial English, all secondary modal verbs converged on a /CVCə/ phonetic template with similar vowels and consonants (15) (cf. Lorenz and Tizón-Couto 2020).

(15)

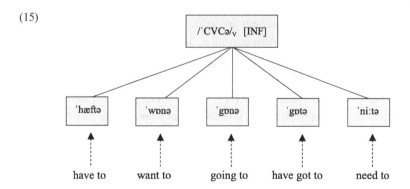

Discussion and research questions. Cognitive linguists agree that constructions vary on a scale of schematicity, but the structure of this scale is not easy to determine. Assuming that a person's knowledge of constructions includes both lexical constructions and constructional schemas, it is reasonable to assume that lexical and schematic constructions are linked by taxonomic relations. Yet many researchers assume that the hierarchical organization of the constructicon involves more than two levels. Argument-structure constructions, for example, are often represented in taxonomies with three levels: (i) frequent lexical chunks including particular verbs and arguments, (ii) verb-specific pivot schemas with open slots for arguments, and (iii) fully schematic constructions including slots for both verbs and arguments (16).

(16)

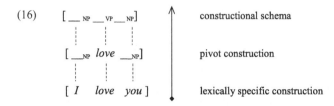

Evidence for the three levels comes from research on L1 acquisition (Braine 1976; Tomasello 2003), but there are many open questions. Most linguistic studies on schematicity concentrate on structural properties of constructions, but schematicity also concerns the meaning of constructions. Moreover, not all linguistic generalizations may be represented in constructional schemas. As we will see in Section 5, there is good evidence that grammar incudes neighborhoods of similar constructions that are not licensed by an overarching schema.

3.2 Sequential Relations

Constructions are automated processing units in which morphemes, words, phrases, and clauses are linked together by sequential relations (Bybee 2010: 33–37; Diessel 2019a: 63–89; Schmid 2020: 235–259). Sequential relations are commonly created by automatization, a domain-general process that affects both motor actions (e.g. dancing, articulation) and cognitive processes (e.g. counting, utterance planning) (Logan 1988). Since sequential processing occurs in time, automatization has a forward direction. When the first element of an automated string is activated, all subsequent elements are also automatically activated with no or little effort and control (Logan 1988). Since automatization is driven by frequency of use, sequential links occur with varying strength. All else being equal, the more frequent a string of linguistic elements, the tighter the associative links between them. This holds for both lexical constructions (e.g. collocations) and constructional schemas (17).

(17)

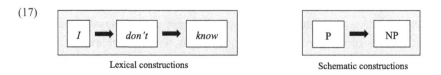

Lexical constructions   Schematic constructions

Table 3 Different types of relational expressions

Word class	Example	Entailed concepts	Typically encoded by
V	*kick*	agent, patient	noun phrase
A	*furry*	animal	noun
P	*under*	location	noun phrase
CONJ	*when*	event, state	clause
DET	*the*	entity	noun
AUX	*will*	action, state	verb

Automatization is of central significance to linear processing, but sequential associations are also shaped by conceptual processes (Diessel 2019a: 175–185). Many words designate semantic relations that entail other concepts. The most prominent example is the verb. Verbs entail semantic participants that are commonly encoded as arguments. Like verbs, adjectives are relational expressions that designate a property or quality of an associated entity. Moreover, most function words are relational expressions that entail other concepts expressed by co-occurring content words, phrases, or clauses. Table 3 provides an overview of various types of relational expressions and the concepts they entail.

Automatization creates forward-oriented sequential links, but the sequential links of relational expressions do not have an inherent direction: They can refer both forwards and backwards depending on their position in a phrase or clause. Individual languages tend to place all relational expressions in parallel positions so that conceptually motivated sequential links typically refer in the same direction. In English, for example, relational expressions tend to create forward-oriented associations as they typically precede the entailed element. In Japanese, however, it is the other way around, that is, in Japanese relational expressions follow the associated element creating backward-oriented sequential associations (18).

(18)

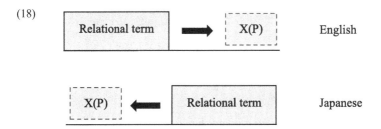

One piece of evidence for forward-oriented sequential links comes from research on sentence processing (Altmann and Mirković 2009). There is a large body of recent results indicating that listeners often anticipate, or predict, elements of an unfolding sentence (Kamide et al. 2003; Kuperberg and Jaeger 2016). For example, Altmann and colleagues conducted a series of experiments in which they observed that listeners often look at a particular referent (in the surrounding situation) before it is mentioned (Altmann and Kamide 1999; Kamide et al. 2003). In one experiment, participants were shown a scene including a boy, a ball, a cake, a toy car, and a toy train (see Figure 1) as they listened to sentences including different verbs, for example *eat* and *move* (19a–b).

(19) a. The boy will eat ... the cake.
      b. The boy will move ... the cake.

All verbs were transitive in this experiment but entailed different semantic types of arguments: *Eat*, for example, entails an edible object, whereas *move* entails any kind of object that can change its location. As expected, Altmann and Kamide (1999) found that, when listeners heard the verb *move*, they randomly looked at all objects of the shown scene; but when they heard *eat*, they looked at the cake before it was mentioned, indicating

Figure 1 Example scene of an experiment shown to participants listening to the sentences in (19a–b) (cf. Altmann and Kamide 1999)

that *eat* created a forward-oriented sequential link to a particular referent (i.e. the cake), leading listeners to anticipate the upcoming object.

In a subsequent study, Kamide et al. (2003) used the same experimental paradigm to investigate sequential processing in Japanese. Since Japanese has OV word order, it is impossible to predict the occurrence of a particular argument from the clause-final verb. Yet Kamide and colleagues hypothesized that listeners of Japanese also anticipate upcoming elements of an unfolding sentence when these elements are predictable from structural or semantic cues. In one experiment, listeners looked at a restaurant scene including a waitress, a customer, a hamburger, and several nonedible objects (see Figure 2) while listening to sentences in which the two initial NPs referred to the waitress and customer. The sentence beginnings were identical except that the second NP occurred in different case forms. In condition 1, the clause-initial subject was followed by an accusative NP; and in condition 2, it was followed by a dative NP (20a–b). Both NP-NP beginnings can be immediately followed by a transitive verb, but they can also occur with another NP before a ditransitive verb.

(20) a. waitress$_{NOM}$ customer$_{ACC}$ ... (NP$_{DAT}$) ... V.
      b. waitress$_{NOM}$ customer$_{DAT}$ ... (NP$_{ACC}$) ... V.

Figure 2 Example scene of an experiment shown to participants listening to the sentences in (20a–b) (cf. Kamide et al. 2003)

Since ditransitive constructions tend to include the dative NP before the direct object (and since dative objects are rare outside of ditransitive constructions in Japanese), Kamide and colleagues hypothesized that listeners would anticipate the occurrence of another referent when the second NP occurred in dative case (20b) but would not anticipate a third referent when the second NP occurred in accusative case (20a). This hypothesis was borne out by the results of their experiment. As expected, listeners did not look at a particular object after an accusative NP but anticipated the hamburger as direct object and theme after a dative NP. Note, however, that while the anticipatory looks in the English study were invoked by conceptual properties of the verb, the Japanese data can only be explained by listeners' experience with automated strings of case-marked NPs.

Discussion and research questions. There is good evidence that automatization creates forward-oriented sequential links regardless of a particular word order. As we have seen, listeners of both head-initial and head-final languages anticipate upcoming elements in the speech stream. However, while the forward-orientation of automatization is likely to be universal, the conceptual links created by relational expressions point in opposite directions in head-initial and head-final languages, suggesting that sequential processing is fundamentally distinct in VO and OV languages (Hawkins 2004). The sources and directionality of sequential associations need to be investigated in more detail. In this short section, I have concentrated on automatization and the conceptual properties of relational terms, but there is good reason to assume that sequential processing is also influenced by discourse-pragmatic factors such as topicality and the flow of consciousness (Chafe 1994). Analyzing the interaction between the various factors that affect the sequential organization of constructions is an important topic for future research.

3.3 Symbolic Relations

Symbolic relations combine form and meaning. They are at the heart of the definition of linguistic signs. Traditionally, linguistic signs are restricted to lexemes, but construction grammar has extended the notion of sign from lexemes to constructions (Section 1). Both are commonly defined as conventional pairings of form and meaning; but, while construction grammar has emphasized the parallels between lexemes and constructions, it is important to recognize that the meanings of lexemes and constructions arise from different conceptual processes.

Linguistic meaning is a multifaceted phenomenon that is studied in two linguistic subfields: semantics and pragmatics. Semantics is concerned with those aspects of meaning that are not influenced by the context, whereas pragmatics is concerned with context-dependent aspects of meaning (Grice 1975). In accordance with this view, Schmid (2020) distinguishes between **symbolic** and **pragmatic associations**. Both types of associations are concerned with meaning, but "pragmatic associations are much wider in scope than symbolic associations, because they include context-dependent information," according to Schmid (2020: 48).

Diessel (2019a: 91–112) takes a somewhat different approach. Following Langacker (1987, 1991, 2008), Diessel argues that there is no principal distinction between semantics and pragmatics, as all aspects of meaning are ultimately created by inferential processes evoked in specific contexts. The whole idea of analyzing meaning without considering usage and context is ill-conceived from a usage-based perspective. Building on research in cognitive psychology (Bates and MacWhinney 1989), Diessel (2019a: 90–112) characterizes linguistic forms as cues or stimuli speakers use to manipulate listeners' mental states in a particular context. The selection and interpretation of linguistic cues involve several interacting processes, including theory-of-mind (or social cognition), conceptualization, and entrenchment. When the same cues are recurrently used in similar situations to accomplish the same goal, they become associated with particular pathways of semantic interpretation that can be seen as symbolic associations. Like other types of associations, symbolic associations are strengthened by entrenchment and stabilized by conventionalization (Schmid 2020).

Different types of linguistic forms evoke different types of symbolic associations. Yet Diessel (2019a: 91–93) claims that all symbolic associations are initially created by (pragmatic) inference and then strengthened and restructured by other cognitive processes. Good evidence for the role of inference in creating symbolic associations comes from research on word learning. In some of the older acquisition literature, it is assumed that children typically learn the meaning of a new word when the intended referent is present and visually accessible to the child. However, as Tomasello and colleagues have shown in a series of experiments, the referent does not have to be co-present to link a new phonetic form to a particular meaning. What is crucial is that children understand a speaker's intention in a particular context. When children are able to make sense of the communicative event, they can easily infer the meaning of a new word, even when the new phonetic form does not appear in the presence of the intended referent or when the referent is not perceptually accessible to the child (for a review of this research, see Tomasello 2003: 43–93).

Word meanings are learned in communicative settings that involve world knowledge, that is, knowledge about social interactions, objects, and people. As a consequence, word meanings are closely related to **encyclopedic knowledge**. According to Langacker (1987), every lexeme is interpreted against the background of a whole network of conceptual knowledge that is grounded in world knowledge (cf. Fillmore 1982: 381). The word *sun*, for example, designates a star that entails the universe or solar system as its background; but the lexeme *sun* also evokes a wide range of other concepts including sky, day, light, heat, summer, vacation, life on earth, the color red (or yellow), and happiness. While one might argue that *sun* has a prototypical meaning (denoting a star), the lexeme *sun* is associated with a wide range of other concepts that are co-activated when *sun* is used in a particular context (21).

(21)

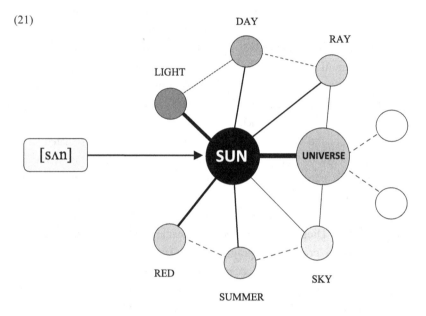

Psycholinguists refer to this phenomenon as a **spreading activation** (Collins and Loftus 1975). Evidence for spreading activation comes from research on lexical priming and other lexical association tasks (Dell 1986). The direction and intensity of activation spreading are determined by three factors: (i) the structure of the conceptual network, (ii) the current context, and (iii) a language user's prior experience with particular linguistic forms (Diessel 2019a: 93–107).

Like lexemes, constructions can be seen as cues or stimuli that evoke particular pathways of semantic interpretation. However, since (schematic) constructions generalize over strings of lexical expressions, they have more abstract meaning than lexemes (i.e. content words). Lexemes provide access to open-ended networks of encyclopedic knowledge (Langacker 1987: 163), but constructions do not target world knowledge. Instead, constructions provide **processing instructions to guide listeners' interpretation of**

lexemes (Diessel 2019a: 107–111). Argument-structure constructions, for example, assign thematic roles to nominal expressions and integrate them into a coherent scene (22).

(22)

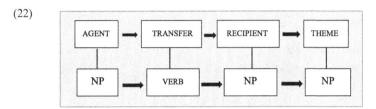

A particularly interesting case of how constructions guide listeners' semantic interpretation of lexemes is the processing of relative clauses. Relative clauses modify a main-clause nominal that serves a particular semanto-syntactic role in the relative clause. If we look at relative clauses from a cross-linguistic perspective, we find many different strategies to guide listeners' interpretation of the relativized referent (i.e. the referent that corresponds to the head noun inside of the relative clause). To begin, many European languages indicate the semanto-syntactic role of the relativized referent by a case-marked relative pronoun, as illustrated by the examples in (23a–d) from German.

(23) German

    a. Der Mann, **der**$_{\text{NOM}}$ …   'The man who …'
    b. Der Mann, **den**$_{\text{ACC}}$ …   'The man whom$_{\text{ACC}}$ …'
    c. Der Mann, **dem**$_{\text{DAT}}$ …   'The man whom$_{\text{DAT}}$ …'
    d. Der Mann, **mit dem**$_{\text{DAT}}$ …   'The man with whom$_{\text{DAT}}$ …'

Like German, English has case-marked relative pronouns, but since the object form *whom* is often replaced by the subject form *who* (notably in American English), case marking is only of minor importance to the formation of English relative clauses. In addition to case marking, English uses several other cues to indicate the relativized role, for example word order, the presence or absence of a relative marker, a dangling or fronted preposition, and the use of different verb forms (present vs. past participle) (24a–f).

(24)   a. The man **who saw us** …
    b. The man **(who) we saw** …
    c. The place **where** she lives …
    d. The ball she played **with** …
    e. The man **writing** a letter …
    f. The letter **written** by John …

Different verb forms are also used in many other languages to indicate the relativized referent. In Turkish, for example, subject relatives include a participle (25a) whereas nonsubject relatives are formed by nominalizations (25b–d). Note that the various nonsubject relatives have the same form in Turkish. As Haig (1998) pointed out, the relative clauses in (25b–d) are structurally equivalent but the head nouns evoke different semantic interpretations.

(25)   Turkish (Haig 1998: 95)

    a. *[Kitab-ı   al-**an**]   öğrenci* ...   AGENT
       book-ACC buy-PTC student
       'The student who bought the book ...'

    b. *[Ben-im yaz-**dığ-ım**]*   *bir mektup* ...   PATIENT
       I-GEN   write-NML-POSS.1SG   a   letter
       'A letter I wrote ...'

    c. *[Ben-im yaz-**dığ-ım**]*   *oda* ...   LOCATION
       I-GEN   write-NML-POSS.1SG   room
       'The room I wrote in ...'

    d. *[Ben-im yaz-**dığ-ım**]*   *kalem* ...   INSTRUMENT
       I-GEN   write-NML-POSS.1SG   pen
       'The pen I wrote with ...'

Generalizing across these observations, we may characterize relative clauses as linear processing units that guide listeners' interpretation of the relativized referent by various types of structural and semantic cues.

Discussion and research questions. Cognitive linguists have analyzed the meanings of both lexemes and constructions in great detail, but they usually look at meaning from a static perspective. What is needed is a dynamic theory of usage-based semantics in which meaning is derived from language use.

The definition of constructions as signs has led researchers to emphasize the parallels between lexemes and constructions. Both are commonly described as conventional pairings of form and meaning; but while the sign-based view of linguistic structure is foundational to the constructivist approach, it is important to recognize that lexemes and schemas have different semantic properties. Lexemes prompt listeners to derive rich semantic interpretations from a conceptual network that is related to world knowledge, whereas constructional schemas serve to guide listeners' interpretation of lexical material. Lexemes and schemas invoke, thus, different conceptual processes. However, if we think of the constructicon as a continuum of linguistic signs, ranging from simple lexemes to highly abstract schemas, the two processes are often combined in (item-specific) constructions. More research is needed to examine the conceptual processes that are evoked by the many different types of lexemes and constructions (for a recent study of constructional semantics, see Willich 2022).

3.4 Filler-Slot Relations

Filler-slot relations are associations that connect the slots of constructional schemas with particular lexical or phrasal fillers. Filler-slot relations are of central significance to the analysis of word classes and other grammatical categories. We will consider the network approach to grammatical categories in Section 4. Here, we focus on some general properties of filler-slot associations in different types of constructions.

Every (schematic) construction includes at least one slot that is associated with a class of lexical and/or phrasal fillers. Argument-structure constructions, for example, include slots for nominal and verbal fillers. Traditionally, filler-slot relations are analyzed in terms of matching categories (Goldberg 1995; Fillmore and Kay 1999). On this view, a lexeme can be combined with a construction if it fits the syntactic and semantic specifications of a particular slot in a constructional schema. In the case of argument structure, verbs select particular participant roles and constructions provide slots for certain argument fillers. If a particular verb and a particular argument-structure construction specify the same roles, they can fuse. This is stated in Goldberg's (1995, 2006) **Semantic Coherence Principle**:

> The Semantic Coherence Principle ensures that the participant roles of the verb and the argument roles of the construction must be semantically compatible. (Goldberg 2006: 40)

There is abundant evidence that verbs and argument-structure constructions usually specify the same roles (Stefanowitsch and Gries 2003); but the Semantic Coherence Principle is too rigid. As many researchers have pointed out, argument-structure constructions abound with lexical idiosyncrasies that are not predictable from semantic criteria (Boas 2003, 2010; Herbst 2014; see also Goldberg 1995: 129–132). For example, English has two constructions denoting transfer, that is, the double-object construction (e.g. *He gave Jack the book*) and *to*-dative construction (e.g. *He gave the book to Jack*). Both constructions occur with transfer verbs, denoting physical or communicative transfer (e.g. *give, tell*); but there are some well-known idiosyncrasies. The verb *forgive*, for example, appears in the double-object construction although *forgive* does not express any sense of transfer (26a); and the verb *donate* does not appear in the double-object construction (in standard American English) despite the fact that *donate* is a typical transfer verb (26b). Note, however, that *donate* appears in the *to*-dative construction, for example *She donated money to a charity organization*.

(26)   a. She **forgave** me my mistakes.
       b. *She **donated** a charity organization money.

The vast majority of transfer verbs alternate between the double-object and *to*-dative constructions, but many verbs are biased in their distribution. *Offer*, for example, appears more frequently in the double-object construction than statistically expected, whereas *bring* tends to occur in the *to*-dative construction (Gries and Stefanowitsch 2004). Similar biases and idiosyncrasies have been observed with many other argument-structure constructions (e.g. Pinker 1989; Goldberg 1995; Boas 2003, 2010; Perek 2015; van Lier and Messerschmidt 2022). For example, many (in)transitive verbs alternate between causative and inchoative uses (Haspelmath et al. 2014). *Open*, for example, can be used as an inchoative verb in the intransitive construction (27a) and as a causative verb in the transitive construction (27b).

(27)　　a.　The door **opened**.
　　　　b.　He **opened** the door.

The alternation between causative and inchoative verbs is very common in English (28–31), but most verbs are statistically skewed in their distribution. *Improve*, for example, is primarily used as an inchoative verb in the intransitive construction, whereas *break* is mainly used as a causative verb in the transitive construction (Haspelmath et al. 2014). Moreover, some verbs that are semantically similar to the verbs of the causative-inchoative alternation are confined to one or the other use. *Disappear*, for example, is exclusively used in intransitive clauses (32), whereas *create* is restricted to the transitive construction (33).

(28)　　a.　The situation **improved**.
　　　　b.　He **improved** the situation.

(29)　　a.　The glass **broke**.
　　　　b.　He **broke** the glass.

(30)　　a.　The cloths **dried**.
　　　　b.　He **dried** the cloths.

(31)　　a.　The ice **melted**.
　　　　b.　The sun **melted** the ice.

(32)　　a.　The problem **disappeared**.
　　　　b.　*He **disappeared** the problem.

(33)　　a.　*A monster **created**.
　　　　b.　He **created** a monster.

Both the statistical biases and idiosyncrasies of verbs and argument-structure constructions are not (fully) predictable from semantic criteria. There is, for example, no obvious semantic reason why *disappear* cannot be used as a causative verb, given that *disappear* can occur in periphrastic causative constructions (cf. *He made it disappear*); and there is also no obvious reason why semantically similar verbs, such as *dry* and *melt*, are (often) differently skewed in their distribution (Haspelmath et al. 2014). Something is missing in this account. It is simple but crucial to the network approach: Irrespective of any semantic criteria, speakers associate particular verbs with particular constructions based on their experience with these expressions. If this is correct, it is reasonable to assume that argument structure includes associative connections between individual verbs and particular constructions (34).

(34)

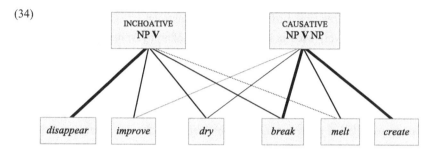

Good evidence for filler-slot associations comes from psycholinguistic research on sentence processing. Early research on sentence processing paid little attention to lexical expressions, but there is now a large body of research indicating that syntactic processing is guided by language users' experience with particular lexemes. For example, Trueswell (1996) showed that the processing of passive relative clauses varies with the relative frequency with which individual verbs occur in passive voice: Verbs such as *consider*, which are frequently used in passive voice, facilitate the processing of passive relatives (35a), whereas verbs such as *want*, which are only rarely used in passive voice, make passive relatives more difficult to process (35b). Similar effects of lexical frequency on sentence processing have been found in many other studies (for a review, see MacDonald and Seidenberg 2006).

(35)   a. The applicant **considered** by the committee …
       b. The applicant **wanted** by the committee …

Further evidence for filler-slot associations comes from research on structural priming. Like lexemes, constructions are more easily activated when they are primed by a preceding construction. A passive sentence, for example, is more easily activated when it is primed by another passive sentence in the previous discourse (for a review, see Pickering and Ferreira 2008). However, while structural priming is in principle independent of words, the priming effect is greatly enhanced if the structural prime includes the same lexemes as the prime target, for example the same verb. Pickering and Branigan (1998) called this the "lexical boost" of structural priming, which they analyzed within a network model in which lexemes and constructions are connected by filler-slot relations.

Filler-slot relations are not restricted to verbs and argument-structure constructions. They also occur with other types of lexemes and constructions (Diessel 2020). For example, adjectives are associated with two main constructions in English: (i) noun phrases (e.g. *a big tree*) and (ii) copular clauses (e.g. *the tree is big*). Most English adjectives occur in both types of constructions, but there are some well-known lexical idiosyncrasies. *Utter*, for example, is restricted to the attribute construction, whereas *afraid* and *sure* are exclusively used in copular clauses. Moreover, many adjectives are skewed in their frequency distribution. *Long* and *little*, for example, are statistically biased to appear in the attribute construction, whereas *impossible* and *awesome* are biased to occur in copular clauses. While researchers have often argued that these patterns are semantically motivated (Bybee and Thompson 2022), it seems unlikely that semantic factors alone can explain the distribution of particular adjectives across the two constructions. There is, for example, no obvious semantic reason why *afraid* is restricted to copular clauses given that semantically similar adjectives such as *anxious* and *frightened* are commonly used as nominal attributes. One way to explain the statistical biases and constraints in the distribution of adjectives is that language users associate individual adjectives with particular constructions based on their experience with these expressions in language use. The network diagram in (36) illustrates how six selected adjectives are linked to the two major adjective constructions of English by weighted filler-slot relations.

(36)

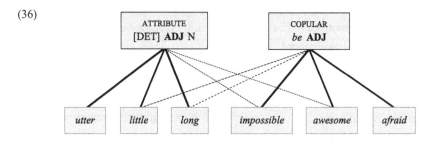

Discussion and research questions. In sum, filler-slot relations are determined by two general factors: (i) the semantic compatibility of particular lexemes and slots and (ii) language users' experience with specific co-occurrence patterns of lexemes and constructions. Early research in construction grammar has focused on semantic factors for analyzing the interaction between lexemes and constructions (Goldberg's Semantic Coherence Principle), but it is language users' experience with particular co-occurrence patterns that motivates the network account.

In the default case, speakers select lexical expressions that fit the semantic specifications of a particular slot; but, as we have seen, there are many idiosyncrasies that are unpredictable from semantic criteria. Most of these idiosyncrasies are the result of language change. For example, earlier in the section it was noted that, although *forgive* does not denote transfer, it appears in the double-object construction (which indicates transfer). Synchronically, *forgive* does not fit the semantic profile of the double-object construction; but in Old English *forgiefan* meant 'give' or 'grant', suggesting that the semantic mismatch of Present Day English is the result of lexical change (Goldberg 1995: 132). Similarly, many Romance verbs donating transfer (e.g. *donate, contribute, explain*) are restricted to the *to*-dative construction for historical reasons. In Old English, transfer events were almost exclusively expressed by the double-object construction. The *to*-dative emerged only later under French and Latin influence and it seems that many Romance transfer verbs entered English via the *to*-dative construction and have never been extended to the double-object construction despite their meaning (Colleman and De Clerck 2011; Zehnenter 2019).

The diachronic development of filler-slot associations is of central significance to the study of grammar emergence in the usage-based approach. There are some pioneering studies on constructional change that are concerned with filler-slot associations (Israel 1996; Colleman and De Clerck 2011; Traugott and Trousdale 2013; Hilpert 2013, 2021; Hoffmann 2019; Zehnenter 2019; Bouso 2020). However, more research is needed to understand how the associations between lexemes and constructions evolve and change.

Closely related to the development of filler-slot associations is the issue of linguistic **productivity** (Goldberg 2006, 2019). In formal grammar, linguistic productivity is explained by algorithmic rules that combine lexemes and categories to composite structures. In the usage-based approach, however, productivity is commonly defined as the propensity of a schema to be extended to novel items (Langacker 2000: 26; Bybee 2010: 94). On this account, type and token frequency have a significant impact on linguistic productivity. If we think of constructions as networks, type and token frequency can be modeled by filler-slot relations. To simplify, the more lexical fillers are linked to a particular slot, and the stronger the associative connections between them, the higher is the productivity of that slot. The network view of constructions sheds new light on linguistic productivity, but the approach has not yet been worked out in detail (for a review and some new suggestions, see Diessel 2019a: 126–141).

3.5 Horizontal Relations

Finally, horizontal relations are associations between constructions at the same level of abstraction. Since horizontal relations are the main focus of Section 5, the current section is confined to a few general remarks. Horizontal relations have been proposed in several recent studies to describe associations between similar and contrastive constructions (Cappelle 2006; Van de Velde 2014; Perek 2015; Booij and Audring 2017; Lyngfelt et al. 2018; Audring 2019; Diessel 2019a; Diewald 2020; Sommerer and Smirnova 2020; Bloom 2021; Hilpert 2021; Ungerer 2021). Let us consider the English verb-particle construction as an example (37a–b) (Cappelle 2006).

(37) a. He turned the radio **on**.
  b. He turned **on** the radio.

As can be seen, the transitive verb-particle construction has two word order variants: (i) verb-object-particle (37a) and (ii) verb-particle-object (37b). The two ordering patterns describe the same scene but tend to occur in different contexts. To simplify, the order V-NP-PART is preferred with short, pronominal objects denoting a familiar referent, whereas the order V-PART-NP is preferred with long, lexical objects denoting a new referent (Gries 2003). In generative grammar, the two ordering patterns are derived from the same underlying representation. The derivational account emphasizes the commonalities between the two patterns but pays little attention to the differences between them. Construction grammar has abandoned syntactic derivations and has emphasized the semantic and pragmatic differences between formally related constructions (see Section 5). In accordance with this view, Gries analyzed the two word order patterns of the verb-particle construction as two separate constructions "that do not form a single category" (Gries 2003: 141). Considering both accounts, Cappelle (2006) maintained that an adequate analysis of the verb-particle construction needs to explain both the similarities and differences between the two word order patterns. In order to account for their shared properties, Cappelle proposed a high-level schema with "underspecified word order" that subsumes the two ordering patterns as subconstructions; and in order to account for the differences between them, he proposed a "relatedness link" that characterizes them as complementary constructions. On this account, the verb-particle construction involves both taxonomic and horizontal relations (38) (from Cappelle 2006).

(38)

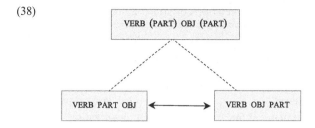

Similar analyses have been proposed for other pairs of related constructions (e.g. Perek 2015). There is growing consensus among constructivist scholars that the constructicon needs horizontal relations in order to explain how constructions evolve and change (Van de Velde 2014; Sommerer and Smirnova 2020; Bloom 2021). Nevertheless, the nature of these relations is not yet fully understood. We will discuss and elaborate the various proposals regarding horizontal relations in Section 5. Here, we note that every construction has a particular ecological location in the grammar network that is defined by its relationship to other constructions with similar forms and meanings (Section 5).

3.6 Conclusion

To briefly sum up the discussion in this section, constructions are usually described as atomic nodes of symbolic networks (or taxonomies). Yet a number of recent studies have questioned this view, arguing that constructions are multidimensional entities that are better analyzed as networks. In this section, we have considered five different types of associative relations that concern different dimensions of constructions. Each relation has particular properties that are shaped by domain-general cognitive processes. Table 4 summarizes the main points of the previous discussion.

4 Syntactic Categories as Networks

In traditional and generative grammar, syntactic structure is derived from two basic components: (i) a small set of primitive categories functioning as syntactic building blocks and (ii) concatenating rules that combine the syntactic building blocks to composite structures. Construction grammar has replaced concatenating rules by constructions, or schemas, but has maintained syntactic categories. Most constructivist scholars agree that, while rules should be replaced by schemas, grammatical analysis needs syntactic categories such as noun, verb, and subject. However, if linguistic structure is licensed by constructions rather than by rules, what is the nature of syntactic categories? Where do categories such as noun, verb, and subject come from? And how do they relate to the notion of construction?

Table 4 Associative relations of constructions

Associations	Elements they combine	Domain-general processes
Taxonomic	constructions at different levels of abstraction	schematization, categorization
Sequential	linguistic items in linear order	automatization, conceptualization
Symbolic	form and meaning	conceptualization, social cognition
Filler-slot	slots of constructions and lexical or phrasal fillers	semantic fit, entrenchment
Horizontal	constructions at the same level of abstraction	analogy, conceptualization

These questions are only rarely addressed in the constructivist approach but are center stage in **Radical Construction Grammar**, a variety of cognitive construction grammar developed by Croft (2001) (see Section 2.2). Challenging the traditional view of syntactic categories as primitive concepts or building blocks, Croft (2001: 4) argued that "constructions are the basic units of syntactic representation, and that categories are derived from the construction(s) in which they appear." Croft turns the traditional method of syntactic analysis upside down. Traditionally, syntactic structures are defined in terms of word classes and grammatical relations, but in Radical Construction Grammar it is the other way around, that is, word classes and relations are defined in terms of constructions:

> Constructions, not categories and relations, are the basic, primitive units of syntactic representation. The categories and relations found in constructions are derivative. (Croft 2001: 46)

Croft's main argument for rejecting the traditional view of syntactic categories as primitive concepts comes from research on language variation. If syntactic categories were primitive concepts, one would expect them to be similar, or even identical, across both languages and constructions. However, many decades of linguistic research have shown that grammar exhibits an enormous amount of structural variation, both across and within languages. Typologists have shown that languages differ so radically from one another "that it is very hard to find any single structural property they share" (Evans and Levinson 2009: 429); and corpus linguists have shown that, contrary to what is commonly assumed, syntactic categories are not uniform across registers and constructions (Biber et al. 1999).

In accordance with the usage-based model, Radical Construction Grammar characterizes grammatical categories as emergent concepts. However, Croft's claim that constructions are "primitive units" of syntactic representation is potentially misleading. While constructions are crucial to explain the emergence of word-class categories and grammatical relations, they are not primitive units. Like all other aspects of grammar, constructions are emergent concepts shaped by language use (as explained in Section 3).

In what follows, we will consider network accounts for three basic syntactic concepts: (i) word classes, (ii) phrasal constituents, and (iii) grammatical relations. It is argued that these concepts are inextricably related to constructions. They emerge within the same networks as constructional schemas and involve the same types of associations.

4.1 Word Classes

Word classes, also known as parts of speech, are at the heart of traditional syntactic theory. They are commonly divided into two basic types: **content words** and **function words**. Content words comprise the vast majority of lexical items that express the semantic core of an utterance. Function words are a much smaller class of items that serve abstract grammatical functions. The current section is concerned with content words; grammatical function words will be considered in Section 4.2 on phrasal constituents.

Content words are commonly divided into three major word classes: nouns, verbs, and adjectives. In traditional grammar, each word class is associated with a particular semantic function: Nouns designate entities, verbs designate actions, and adjectives designate properties. In addition, word classes are commonly defined by structural criteria, such as the occurrence of particular affixes or function words. The semantic and structural criteria correlate with each other, but there are many idiosyncrasies (i.e. exceptions), making it difficult to define nouns, verbs, and adjectives by both types of criteria. Formal grammar prioritizes structural criteria for defining word classes. In this approach, nouns, verbs, and adjectives are pure syntactic categories that are only indirectly related to meaning. Functional linguists have taken a different approach. They often define nouns, verbs, and adjectives as semantic prototypes that motivate the occurrence of certain structural properties (Hopper and Thompson 1984). However, while the prototype approach can explain, to some extent, why the structural features of word classes do not always coincide with their meanings, there remain many open questions. In particular, the (traditional) prototype approach does not explain how word-class categories arise and change. If nouns, verbs, and adjectives are not primitive concepts, as usage-based linguists claim, we need a theory that explains how nouns, verbs, and adjectives derive from usage. In what follows, I present a dynamic network account for the three major word classes in which nouns, verbs, and adjectives are emergent categories that arise from the interaction between lexemes and constructions (Croft 1991, 2001; Diessel 2019a, 2020).

Traditionally, word class categories are regarded as properties of individual lexemes. Every lexeme is assigned to a particular word class that is specified in the lexicon (e.g. *tree* is a noun). However, one can also think of nouns, verbs, and adjectives in terms of structural positions. Constructions include slots for lexemes of particular word classes. These slots occur in three different types of constructions: (i) morphological constructions, which include slots that are specified by particular affixes, (ii) phrasal constructions, which include slots that are marked by particular function words, and (iii) clausal constructions, which include slots that are defined by particular configurations of phrasal constituents (39).

(39)

	MORPHOLOGICAL CONSTRUCTIONS	PHRASAL CONSTRUCTIONS	CLAUSAL CONSTRUCTIONS
VERBS	[__]-*ed*	AUX [__]	NP [__] NP
NOUNS	[__]-*s*	DET [__]	[__] V
ADJECTIVES	[__]-*est*	ADV [__]	NP *be* [__]

The three types of constructions are historically related by grammaticalization: The inflectional affixes of morphological constructions are commonly derived from function words of phrasal constructions, which in turn are often based on content words of clausal constructions. We will consider some aspects of this development in Section 4.2. Here, we note that the slots for nouns, verbs, and adjectives are not just structural positions but also have meaning. These meanings have been described in two important studies by Croft (1991) and Langacker (1991).

Croft (1991: 59–100) argued that the major word classes are associated with particular speech act functions. Building on Searle (1969), Croft assumes that utterances (or speech acts) include two basic propositional acts: (i) the "act of reference," which serves to identify an entity, and (ii) the "act of predication," which serves to describe the designated entity. The two propositional acts map onto nouns and verbs, or more specifically, they map onto the slots for nouns and verbs, which I call N/V-schemas (Diessel 2019a: 145–148): Lexemes that are used in **N-schemas** perform an act of reference, and lexemes that are used in **V-schemas** perform an act of predication. The distinction between reference and predication is foundational to human communication and likely to be universal (Searle 1969). In addition, Croft proposed a third type of propositional act to characterize adjectives, or **A-schemas**. Specifically, he claimed that while predicative adjectives (e.g. *is old*) serve as predications (similar to intransitive verbs), attributive adjectives (e.g. *old man*) serve a special speech act function, which Croft called "act of modification."

Complementary to Croft's analysis, Langacker (1991) argued that the three major word-class schemas give rise to different construals. The term "construal" refers to the cognitive structuring of information. Every lexeme evokes semantic information, but this information is construed in different ways by different schemas. N-schemas construe a lexeme as a "thing," V-schemas construe a lexeme as a "process," and A-schemas construe a lexeme as a "property." Langacker uses the notions of thing, process, and property as technical terms for general semantic concepts that are distinguished by two criteria: temporality and relatedness. **Things** are atemporal and non-relational, **processes** are temporal and relational, and **properties** are atemporal and relational. To illustrate, the lexeme *hammer* typically occurs in N-schemas, where it is construed as a thing (e.g. *A hammer is a tool*); but *hammer* can also appear in a V-schema, where it is construed as a process (e.g. *He hammered the nail into the wall*). Adjectives, or A-schemas, share properties with both N-schemas and V-schemas. Like syntactic verbs, A-schemas are relational as they entail another concept (namely the modified referent); and like syntactic nouns, A-schemas are atemporal. Table 5 provides a summary of the semantic and pragmatic specifications that Croft (1991) and Langacker (1991) proposed to characterize N/V/A-schemas (see also Croft 2001: 86–88 and Langacker 2008: 103–117).

The three major word-class schemas typically occur with lexical expressions that are semantically compatible with their semantic and pragmatic specifications. As Croft (1991: 88–90) showed, across languages, syntactic nouns (or N-schemas) tend to occur with lexemes denoting objects or animate beings (e.g. *house, boy*); syntactic verbs (or V-schemas) tend to occur with lexemes denoting actions or states (e.g. *run, sit*); and syntactic adjectives (or A-schemas) tend to occur with lexemes denoting properties or qualities (e.g. *tall, intelligent*). The co-occurrence of lexemes and word-class schemas is semantically motivated, but there are numerous exceptions. In all of the languages Croft examined, there were action lexemes

Table 5 Semantic and pragmatic properties of word-class schemas

	N-schemas	**V-schemas**	**A-schemas**
speech act functions	reference	predication	modification
construals	thing [-relation, -temp]	process [+relation, +temp]	property [+relation, -temp]

that occurred in N-schemas and A-schemas (40a–b), object lexemes that occurred in V-schemas and A-schemas (40c–d), and property lexemes that occurred in N-schemas and V-schemas (40e–f).

(40)   a. take a **walk**   Action lexeme in N-schema
        b. **change**able weather   Action lexeme in A-schema
        c. **mail** a message   Object lexeme in V-schema
        d. a **heart**less person   Object lexeme in A-schema
        e. support the **poor**   Property lexeme in N-schema
        f. **modern**ize the house   Property lexeme in V-schema

The examples in (40a–f) illustrate that word-class membership is not strictly predictable from semantic criteria. Even if we define nouns, verbs, and adjectives as semantic prototypes (Hopper and Thompson 1984), it is impossible to predict the distribution of individual lexemes. There is, for instance, no obvious semantic reason why a property term such as *poor* can be used as a syntactic noun, whereas the vast majority of (English) property terms are never used in N-schemas; or why a lexeme such as *sports*, which designates an action, is almost exclusively used as a syntactic noun (but note the expression *He sports a beard*). In order to account for these idiosyncrasies, we need to consider the influence of usage frequency on word-class categorization. Irrespective of any semantic factors, speakers know the word-class functions of lexemes such as *poor* and *sports* because of their experience with these expressions. What is more, speakers do not only know the word-class categories of individual lexemes; they also know that multi-categorical expressions such as *bridge* (N/V) and *open* (V/A) occur with different frequencies as nouns, verbs, and adjectives, suggesting that word-class membership is shaped by frequency of use (MacDonald et al. 1994; Trueswell 1996). In order to account for this, we may use weighted filler-slot relations that are determined by two general factors: (i) the semantic fit between lexemes and schemas and (ii) language users' experience with particular combinations of individual lexemes and schemas (41) (Diessel 2019a: 148–153).

(41)

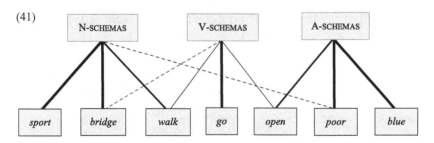

The same approach can be applied to the subclasses of nouns, verbs, and adjectives. Nouns, for example, are commonly divided into count nouns and mass nouns.

Traditionally, mass nouns are defined as a particular semantic class of lexical nouns, but mass nouns are also licensed by a particular word-class schema. The mass noun schema is formally distinct from the count noun schema (e.g. by the absence of indefinite articles) and evokes a different semantic interpretation: The count noun schema construes a lexeme as a discrete entity, but the mass noun schema construes a lexeme as an undifferentiated substance (42a–b).

(42) a. Joe baked **a cake**.
      b. Joe likes **cake**.

The two N-schemas for count nouns and mass nouns are associated with different semantic types of expressions that are compatible with their semantic specifications: Count noun schemas tend to occur with lexemes that designate objects or animate beings, whereas mass noun schemas tend to occur with lexemes that designate substances or abstract concepts (43).

(43)

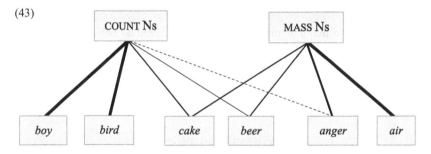

Lexemes that are not compatible with the semantic specifications of a particular noun schema are **coerced** into a novel interpretation, as illustrated by the sentences in (44a–b) in which two prototypical count nouns denoting entities are construed as abstract concepts.

(44) a. You get **a lot of car** for your cash.
      b. There is not **enough train** in America.

Interestingly, while filler-slot associations are usually motivated by semantic factors, they can also be influenced by phonetic features. The formation of English past tense verbs, for example, involves phonetically motivated filler-slot associations. The vast majority of English verbs are formed by the suffix -*ed*; but in addition to the regular past tense, there are several irregular past tense schemas that are characterized by phonetic features. The verbs *sing* and *ring*, for example, are associated with a past tense schema that includes one or more consonants in the onset, the vowel [æ], and a velar nasal in the coda ([CCæŋ]). This schema is so deeply entrenched in memory that it can license the formation of novel past tense forms. To illustrate, given a nonce verb such as *spling*, speakers are not unlikely to produce the past tense form *splang*, in lieu of the regular *splinged*, because *spling* is phonetically similar to *sing* and *ring* (Bybee and Modor 1983). There are several other phonetically specified past tense schemas that compete for activation in usage and development (45). The competition between the various past tense schemas gives rise to overgeneralization errors in L1 acquisition (Diessel 2013) and has been modeled, many times, in computer simulations with neural networks (Elman et al. 1996).

(45)

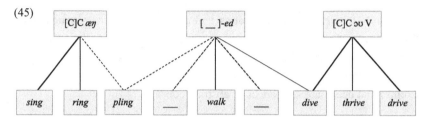

In sum, the three major word classes can be analyzed as networks in which individual lexemes are linked to particular schemas. The associative links are semantically motivated but not strictly predictable from semantic criteria so that speakers have to learn them from their experience with particular co-occurrence patterns of lexemes and word-class schemas.

4.2 Phrasal Constituents

Words that belong to certain word-class categories are grouped together to phrases. In formal grammar, a phrase is a syntactic unit formed by concatenating rules (e.g. NP → DET N). Construction grammar has replaced phrase structure rules by constructional schemas. In this approach, syntactic phrases are linguistic signs that are linked together in networks (Langacker 1997, 2008). In the following, I first describe the conceptual foundations of syntactic constituents and then consider the influence of several other domain-general processes on phrase structure.

4.2.1 The Conceptual Foundations of Constituency

A grammatical phrase typically consists of two elements: a head and a dependent category. In generative grammar, head and dependent are formal syntactic categories, but Langacker (2008: 193–207) argues that (syntactic) heads are also conceptual units. The head is the word-class category that determines the basic properties of a phrase. A noun phrase, for example, is usually organized around a noun that determines the properties of the whole phrase. Like simple nouns, noun phrases designate a thing (in Langacker's 1991 sense of the term; see Section 4.1), serve to perform an act of reference (as described by Croft 1991; see Section 4.1), and are commonly marked by nominal function morphemes, for example determiners and case affixes (Hopper and Thompson 1984).

All phrasal constructions include a relational term that entails (at least) one other expression. The relational term is either the head of the phrase or a dependent category (Langacker 1997). Verbs, for example, are relational heads that entail semantic participants known as complements. Like verbs, adjectives are relational terms that entail other expressions (see Section 2.3), but unlike verbs, adjectives are modifiers, or dependent categories, that entail a nominal head as filler. There are thus two different conceptual types of phrasal constructions (Langacker 1991: 174–175): **head-complement constructions**, which include a relational head (e.g. a verb); and **head-modifier constructions**, which include a relational dependent category (e.g. an adjective) (46).

(46)

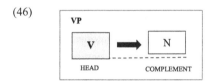 

Like verbs and adjectives, most function words are relational terms that entail other expressions: Determiners entail a noun (47a), prepositions entail a pronoun, noun, or noun phrase (47b), conjunctions entail a clause or proposition (47c), and auxiliaries entail a verb (47d).

(47) a. the → boy
  b. on → the table
  c. after → they left
  d. will → go

Relational expressions can take different types of fillers, for example lexemes, phrases, or (subordinate) clauses. Since (most) nouns are non-relational, they are prototypical fillers. Note, however, that fillers can also be relational terms – a verb, for example, can take another verb as complement.

4.2.2 Automatization

Relational expressions provide the conceptual foundations for NPs, VPs, and PPs, but syntactic constituents are also influenced by automatization. All phrasal constituents include collocations shaped by frequency of use. Examples of different types of collocations are shown in (48).

(48)   NP COLLOCATIONS   VP COLLOCATIONS   PP COLLOCATIONS
        this time   switch on the light under pressure
        the best way   give me a hand   for some reason
        a waste of time   take into account   in the long run

Traditionally, phrase structure analysis abstracts away from individual lexemes and collocations; but in the usage-based approach, phrase structure analysis involves both lexical and schematic phrases. Bybee (2007, 2010) argues that lexical phrases of the same type exhibit different degrees of cohesion if they occur with different frequencies: "the more often particular elements occur together, the tighter the constituent structure" (Bybee 2007: 315). A frequent NP such as *my mother*, for example, is more cohesive than an infrequent NP such as *this hospital*, according to Bybee. Moreover, Bybee claims that, since short lexical phrases are usually more frequent than long lexical phrases, syntactic cohesion varies with the length of syntactic constituents. Other things being equal, a short NP such as *my house* is more cohesive than a long NP such as *my uncle's new house at the sea*. As a consequence, constituent structure is more tightly organized at the bottom of a phrase structure tree than at the top.

Since constructional schemas are derived from strings of lexical expressions, they usually have the same structure as lexical phrases. Yet automatization can give rise to lexical chunks that do not correspond to canonical syntactic phrases. One indication for this are discrepancies between syntactic and phonetic phrasing (Bybee and Scheibman 1999). When automatization accords with conceptualization, syntactic phrases are expressed by phonetically coherent intonation units. As Chafe (1994) and others have shown, pauses and intonation breaks are frequent at phrase boundaries but rare inside of syntactic phrases. However, when automatization and conceptualization do not accord with each other, phonetic phrasing can deviate from canonical phrase structure (Bybee 2010). One well-known example occurs with subject pronouns and auxiliaries in English. Semantically, auxiliaries are related to main verbs, but phonetically, they are often bound to a preceding pronoun and reduced to a clitic, for example *I'll*, *he's*. Since the occurrence of auxiliary clitics correlates with frequency of use (Barth and Kapatsinski 2017), it is reasonable to assume that automatization has given rise to a phonetic phrase that does not match the corresponding structure of an ordinary VP. Thus, Bybee and Scheibman (1999) argued that constituent structure varies between two groupings in NP-AUX-V sequences (cf. 49a–b).

(49)   a.   b.

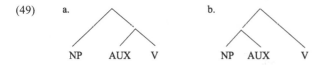

        NP   AUX   V   NP   AUX   V

Similar mismatches between lexical and schematic chunks occur with other types of phrases. For example, Bybee (2007: 330) notes that, while prepositions are usually grouped together with nominal expressions, they can also be linked to other elements. In phrasal verbs, for example, prepositions are associated with the verb (e.g. *look after*). Like contracted auxiliaries, phrasal verbs are lexical chunks that are not consistent with the canonical phrase structure analysis of prepositional phrases (50).

(50)

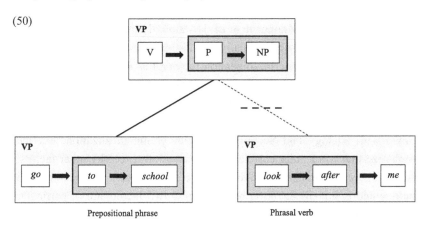

Prepositional phrase   Phrasal verb

4.2.3 Analogy

Automatization and conceptualization create sequential links between head and dependent categories but do not account for constituent order. Constituent order is often variable in sentences but usually fixed in syntactic phrases. In English NPs, for example, determiners, adjectives, and relative clauses occur in fixed structural positions relative to the head noun. The ordering patterns of head and dependent categories vary across languages; but, as Greenberg (1966) and others have shown, there are conspicuous cross-linguistic correlations in word order across syntactic phrases (Dryer 1992).

The discovery of **word order correlations** had a strong impact on syntactic theory, especially in generative grammar. In the aftermath of Greenberg's (1966) seminal study, it has become a standard assumption of generative grammar that the world's languages can be divided into two basic word order types: VO languages, or head-initial languages, in which the head precedes the dependent category in all syntactic phrases; and OV languages, or head-final languages, in which the head follows the dependent category. The VO/OV typology is often described as an empirical generalization; but, as Dryer (1992) and other typologists have pointed out, the typology is incon-sistent. For example, contrary to what is commonly assumed, the order of noun and adjective does not correlate with that of verb and object (Dryer 1988). There are other word order pairs that do not match the VO/OV typology (e.g. the order of noun and demonstratives). Moreover, the phrases that are consistent with the VO/OV typology are often asymmetrical such that one ordering pattern is much more frequent than the other one (Greenberg 1966; Dryer 1992). In accordance with these findings, Justeson and Stephens (1990) showed that a statistical model fits the typological data much better if we assume that the Greenbergian word order correlations consist of locally related word order pairs rather than of two globally distinguished language types (i.e. VO vs. OV or head-initial vs. head-final).

In what follows, I discuss two general factors, that is, analogy and grammaticalization, that explain why syntactic phrases are locally related and why the group of correlating phrases can be interpreted as a network of horizontally related constructions (Diessel 2019a: 175–188). The current section is concerned with analogy and Section 4.2.4 with grammaticalization. Let me emphasize that word order correlations are also influenced by other factors, notably by genetic inheritance and language contact. Here, I concentrate on analogy and grammaticalization because these two factors are of particular importance to the network organization of phrasal constituents.

Analogy is a domain-general process that is often characterized as "structure mapping" (Gentner 1983). There is good evidence in psycholinguistics that speakers map word order patterns across phrasal constructions. For example, Culbertson et al. (2012) conducted a learning experiment to investigate the emergence of word order correlations in syntactic NPs. Participants were exposed to an artificial language including nouns, numerals, and adjectives that were arranged in different orders in different experimental conditions. As expected, the researchers found that the proportions of harmonic word orders (i.e. orders in which adjectives and numerals occur in parallel positions relative to the noun) increased in frequency in the course of the experiment, indicating a "regularization bias" that is arguably motivated by structure mapping or analogy.

The results of the Culbertson study are consistent with what we find in the typological data. Earlier it was noted that the order of noun and adjective does not correlate with that of verb and object. However, while NPs including adjectives are not consistent with the VO/OV typology, there is a cross-linguistic tendency to align the position of adjectives with that of other noun modifiers, for example numerals, genitives, relative clauses (Dryer 1988), which is readily explained if we assume that analogy is the driving force behind the emergence of parallel word orders in similar types of constructions.

Note that while NPs including adjectives are not consistent with the VO/ OV typology, some other types of noun modifiers participate in this typology. In particular, the order of noun and relative clause correlates with that of verb and object (Dryer and Haspelmath 2013). On the face of it, NPs including relative clauses have little in common with VPs including objects. Yet, on closer inspection, we find that these constructions are related by a bridging construction consisting of a verb and a complement clause (Schmidtke-Bode and Diessel 2017). Like relative clauses, complement clauses are subordinate clauses that are often expressed by similar types of constructions (51a–b); and like object NPs, complement clauses are objects that often appear with the same complement-taking verbs as nominal objects (52a–b).

(51)   a. John saw [that the train arrived on platform 3].
        b. John saw [the train [that arrived on platform 3]].

(52)   a. Bill saw [the train].
        b. Bill saw [the train is leaving].

Since complement clauses are similar to both relative clauses and object NPs, there is a tendency to place all three constituents in parallel positions relative to their respective heads, creating a group, or chain, of locally related word order constructions (53).

(53)

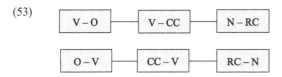

4.2.4 Grammaticalization

Analogy is a powerful mechanism that can affect all kinds of phrases, but in addition to analogy we need to consider grammaticalization in order to explain some of the strongest word order correlations, namely those that include a grammatical function word (Bybee 2010; Dryer 2019). In order to understand this correlation, we must distinguish between **compound phrases** and **grammatical phrases** (Diessel 2019a: 173–188). Compound phrases include two lexical units, whereas grammatical phrases include a lexical unit and a grammatical function word. For example, *father's car* is a compound phrase consisting of two lexical expressions or content words, whereas *a car* is a grammatical phrase consisting of a function word and a content word. Other examples of compound phrases and grammatical phrases are shown in (54).

(54)   COMPOUND PHRASES   GRAMMATICAL PHRASES

[open] [the door]	V-NP	[on] [the table]	P-NP
[go] [into the room]	V-PP	[will] [leave]	AUX-V
[Bill's] [sister]	G-N	[a] [tree]	DET-N
[old] [man]	A-N	[is] [my friend]	COP-NP
[the book] [I read]	N-RC	[if] [it rains]	CONJ-S

Analogy is the main force behind ordering correlations between compound phrases, but ordering correlations that include a grammatical phrase are often created by grammaticalization. The best-known example is the correlation between the order of verb and object and that of verb and auxiliary. As Bybee (2010: 111) and others have noted, tense-aspect auxiliaries are commonly derived from verbs that take another verb as object complement (e.g. *want to leave* → *will leave*). Since verbal complements typically occur in the same position as nominal complements, we find that the emerging auxiliaries precede the main verb in VO languages and that they follow it in OV languages (55).

(55)

VERB – OBJ	OBJ – VERB
want leave	*leave want*
↓	↓
will leave	*leave will*
AUX – VERB	**VERB – AUX**

A similar analysis has been proposed for adpositions (Dryer 2019), but note that adpositions evolve from two main sources: (i) motion and aspectual verbs and (ii) relational nouns and body part terms (Heine et al. 1991). The development of adpositions from motion and aspectual verbs is parallel to that of tense-aspect auxiliaries. In VO languages, verbs develop into prepositions, and in OV languages they develop into postpositions (56).

(56)

VERB – OBJ	OBJ – VERB
give someone	*someone give*
↓	↓
for someone	*someone for*
P – NOUN	**NOUN – P**

The development of adpositions from nouns originates from NPs including a genitive (i.e. nominal) attribute: Nouns that precede a genitive attribute develop into prepositions, and nouns that follow a genitive attribute develop into postpositions (57).

(57)

NOUN – GEN	GEN – NOUN
front place ↓ *in.front.of place*	*place front* ↓ *place in.front.of*
P – NOUN	**NOUN – P**

To give one more example, let us consider the position of subordinate conjunctions in adverbial clauses. In VO languages, subordinate conjunctions tend to occur at the beginning of adverbial clauses, as, for example, in English (*after he left* . . .); but in OV languages, adverbial clauses are often marked by clause-final conjunctions, especially in languages like Japanese in which adverbial clauses consistently precede the main clause (58).

(58)   Japanese (Iwasaki 2013: 269)
        *[Ii   kusuri   o   nonda   **kara**]   sugu   naotta.*
        good   medicine   ACC   drink.PST because   immediately   recover.PST
        '(I) recovered immediately because (I) took some good medicine.'

Adverbial subordinators evolve from many different sources (Hetterle 2015), but most frequently they derive from adpositions. There is a very close connection between adverbial clauses and adpositional phrases that explains why adverbial subordinators and adpositions tend to occur in parallel positions. Since VO languages typically have prepositions, they also often have adverbial clauses marked by initial subordinate conjunctions (e.g. English *after*); and since OV languages typically have postpositions, they also often have adverbial clauses marked by final subordinate conjunctions (Japanese *kara* 'from' [P] > 'because' [SUB]) (59) (for data and other types of developments, see Diessel 2019b).

(59)

P – NOUN	NOUN – P
after dinner ↓ *after we had dinner*	*dinner after* ↓ *we had dinner after*
SUB – S	**S – SUB**

Like analogy, grammaticalization involves particular lexemes and constructions rather than general syntactic rules. Together, analogy and grammaticalization give rise to a network of locally related constructions that one might characterize as a **neighborhood**. A construction neighborhood is an open-ended group of similar constructions that are connected by horizontal relations. We will consider construction neighborhoods in Section 5. Here, we note that the Greenbergian word order correlations can be seen as a network of horizontally related constructions. Summarizing the previous discussion, (60) shows how these constructions are related (if we look at them from a cross-linguistic perspective): Dotted lines indicate (horizontal) relations between constructions that are usually connected by analogy, and arrows indicate (horizontal) relations that are often created by grammaticalization.

(60)

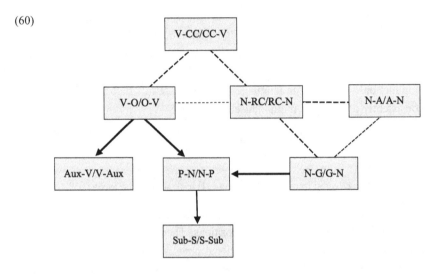

4.2.5 Filler-Slot Relations

Concluding the analysis of syntactic phrases, we need to consider the hierarchical organization of constituency. Many syntactic theories use phrase structure trees to represent the hierarchical structure of sentences. Note that phrase structure trees bear some resemblance with networks. They consist of nodes and arcs, or links, that indicate how the constituents of a sentence are related (61).

(61)

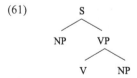

Phrase structure trees are useful to describe some central aspects of syntactic structure, but since they are derived from primitive categories and concatenating rules, they are not consistent with the emergentist view of linguistic structure in the usage-based model. What is needed is a more dynamic network approach that explains how the links between phrasal constituents are shaped by usage (Diessel 2020).

One can think of the links of a phrase structure tree as filler-slot relations. Like lexemes, phrasal constituents are associated with particular slots of constructional schemas. The transitive construction, for example, includes two NP slots for subject and object. In traditional phrase structure grammar, subject and object are represented by the same type of NP, but there are some well-known asymmetries between them. The subject of a transitive clause is usually an animate NP that tends to be shorter and more definite than the object NP. Since formal grammar separates the analysis of syntactic constituency from the analysis of meaning and use, it disregards these asymmetries. However, if we think of linguistic structure in terms of constructions, that is, conventional pairings of form and meaning, we must not ignore that subject and object tend to be expressed by different NPs. Crucially, while the formal differences between subject and object (i.e. in terms of length, definiteness, and internal structure) are motivated by general semantic and discourse-pragmatic factors (i.e. topicality and event structure), there is reason to assume that these differences are also entrenched in memory. In other words, speakers associate the slots of argument-structure constructions with particular phrasal fillers based on their experience with specific co-occurrence patterns.

This does not only hold for subject and object of simple transitive clauses but also for all other syntactic roles. The two object NPs of ditransitive constructions, for example, are associated with very different types of NPs: The NP slot for the indirect object is usually filled by a short lexical NP (or pronoun) denoting an animate referent, whereas the NP slot for the direct object is usually expressed by an inanimate NP that tends to be longer and more topical than the direct object (Bresnan et al. 2007). While these asymmetries are motivated by general semantic factors (Wolk et al. 2013), a number of studies have argued that they are reinforced by frequency of use. For example, Bresnan and Ford (2010) showed that speakers of American and Australian English use ditransitive constructions with somewhat different types of fillers and that this affects the processing of ditransitive sentences in the two varieties, suggesting that the associative relations between constructions and fillers are shaped by language users' experience with particular co-occurrence patterns in different speech communities (for a parallel analysis of New Zealand English, see Bresnan and Hay 2008).

To give one more example, let us consider the effect of experience on object complements in simple transitive clauses (Garnsey et al. 1997). In English, transitive verbs occur with two main types of complements: (i) nominal objects, or NP-complements, and (ii) sentential objects, or S-complements. The occurrence of the two types of complements is semantically motivated. Causative verbs such as *hit* and *kick*, for example, do not take S-complements because their meaning entails an entity rather than an event (as object). Yet communication verbs and verbs of cognition are semantically compatible with both types of complements (62a–b).

(62)   a. I saw someone.
         b. I saw someone was coming.

Note, however, that some communication and cognition verbs do not alternate between these uses. *Want*, for example, is a desiderative verb that does not take finite complement clauses as semantically similar verbs such as *wish* (63a–b); and *think* is a cognition verb that is exclusively used with S-complements, although semantically similar cognition verbs such as *know* and *consider* occur with both S- and NP-complements (64a–b).

(63)   a. I want my money.
         b. *I want that you give me my money.

(64)   a. I think that's a mistake.
         b. *I think a mistake.

What is more, alternating verbs are often skewed in their distribution towards one or the other type of complement. *Find*, for example, is primarily used with NP-complements, whereas *confirm* is more frequent with S-complements than with NP-complements (Wiechmann 2008). Psycholinguists have shown that the statistical biases of alternating verbs influence sentence comprehension and production. When an NP-biased verb such as *find* is combined with an NP-complement, it is processed faster and more often phonetically reduced than when it is combined with an S-complement; but for S-biased verbs, it is the other way around: a verb such as *confirm*, for example, is processed faster and produced with fewer pauses and more phonetic reductions when it is combined with an S-complement than with an NP-complement (Garnsey et al. 1997; Gahl and Garnsey 2004). Since these results are not predictable from general semantic criteria, it seems plausible to assume that they arise from language users' experience with particular co-occurrence patterns, suggesting that the object slots of individual verbs are associated with different types of complements by weighted filler-slot associations (65).

(65)

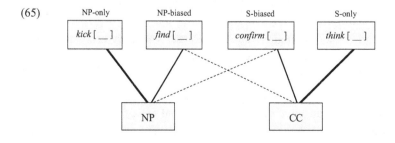

In sum, phrasal constituents are semantically motivated processing units that typically consist of two conceptual elements: (i) a relational term that entails another concept and (ii) a lexical or phrasal filler. The conceptual links between relational terms and fillers are usually strengthened by frequency of use, but automatization can also create associations between lexical expressions that deviate from the semantic associations of canonical phrases. Finally, the various types of phrasal constituents are interrelated. They constitute a network of similar constructions with parallel word orders, similar meanings, and related function words that reflect the influence of two general factors: analogy and grammaticalization.

4.3 Grammatical Relations

Grammatical relations describe the functions of arguments in argument-structure constructions. They are commonly divided into two basic types: subject and object. Traditionally, subject and object are primitive categories of syntactic structure, but Croft (2001) argues that grammatical relations are derived from argument-structure constructions.

Like word classes and phrasal constituents, grammatical relations combine a particular form with meaning. The forms of grammatical relations are defined in terms of various structural properties including word order, case and agreement marking, and behavioral properties such as argument omission and control in complex sentences. Formally defined grammatical relations are called **syntactic functions** (Croft 2001: 203–240).

The semantic properties of grammatical relations are usually described in terms of two general concepts: semantic roles and topicality. **Semantic roles** characterize the participants of verbs and sentences. Every verb entails particular participants (e.g. *drive* entails a driver and a vehicle) that can be grouped together to semantic roles such as agent, patient, experiencer, and theme. Following Fillmore (1968), it is commonly assumed that semantic roles constitute a hierarchy of agentivity ranging from prototypical agents that execute a physical force to prototypical patients that are affected by this force (Croft 2001: 163–165). **Topicality** refers to the activation status of arguments. Like agentivity, topicality constitutes a scale or hierarchy ranging from highly activated discourse participants to new and unfamiliar referents (Chafe 1994). The semantic and pragmatic properties of grammatical relations map onto syntactic functions (Fillmore 1968; Croft 1991). Given a verb with two arguments, the argument that ranks higher on the semantic role hierarchy and the topicality scale is usually encoded as subject and the lower ranked argument as object (66).

(66)

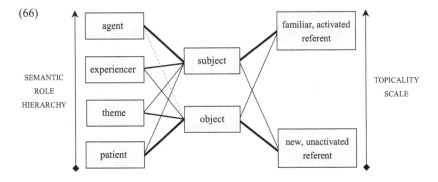

On this account, subject and object are semantically motivated syntactic categories that are formally defined by a set of structural criteria. The semantic motivations for grammatical relations are likely to be universal; but the formal properties of syntactic functions vary across constructions and languages. Consider, for example, the notion of subject. In English, the subject is commonly defined by word order. Usually, the argument that precedes the verb encodes the agent or highest ranked semantic role; but in passive constructions, it is the patient that precedes the verb while the agent is expressed by an optional *by*-phrase (67).

(67)   [The truck]_{PA} was stopped [by the police]_{AG}.

Word order is the most prominent property of subjecthood in English, but not all argument-structure constructions include the subject before the verb. In sentences including a direct quote or locational adjunct, the subject can follow the main verb (68a–b).

(68)   a. "Oops!," said the President.
        b. On the table stood two jellies, one red and one yellow.

Apart from word order, there are several other structural features that characterize the syntactic notion of subject in English: verb agreement (in present tense), case marking (in personal pronouns), and control (in complex sentences). Usually, all of these features co-occur, but there are some well-known idiosyncrasies. Control, for example, has construction- and verb-specific properties. To illustrate, nonfinite adverbial clauses are controlled by the main clause subject (69a), but nonfinite complement clauses occur with both subject and object control. The majority of nonfinite complement clauses are controlled by the object (69b), but sentences including *promise* as main verb occur with subject control (69c).

(69)   a. **John**_i studied hard ___ i to pass the exam.
        b. John convinced **me**_i ___ i to join them.
        c. **John**_i promised ___ i to help us.

Similar construction- and verb-specific idiosyncrasies characterize syntactic functions in other languages. For example, Icelandic has psych-verb constructions in which the highest ranked argument occurs in dative case, which usually marks the indirect object (Barðdal 2006); and Turkish has subordinate clauses that include genitive subjects instead of nominative NPs (Haig 1998). Moreover, in many languages the direct object is not consistently encoded: It occurs with different case markers, or no marker, and can often appear in different structural positions depending on the verb or general semantic and pragmatic properties such as agentivity and definiteness (Schmidtke-Bode and Levshina 2018).

Finally, while the majority of languages encode the single argument of an intransitive clause in the same way as the highest ranked argument of a transitive clause, there are other patterns of argument alignment. In languages with ergative-absolutive marking, the single argument of an intransitive clause is encoded in the same way as the lower ranked argument of a transitive clause; and in languages with split intransitivity, intransitive verbs occur with two formally distinct types of arguments that pattern with one or the other argument of a transitive clause (Dixon 1994). Moreover, the alignment patterns are often expressed by different formal strategies that do not always accord, as in the following example from Nepali (70) in which case marking exhibits an ergative-absolutive pattern whereas agreement marking occurs with nominative-accusative alignment.

(70)   Nepali (Bickel 2011: 400)

   a. *Ma*   *ga-ē̃.*
      1SG.NOM   go-1SG.PST
      'I went.'

   b. *Mai-le*   *timro*   *ghar*   *dekh-ē̃.*
      1SG.ERG   your   house.NOM   see-1SG.PST
      'I saw your house.'

In general, syntactic functions vary across languages and constructions. Considering this variation, Croft (2001) proposed a revision of the traditional definition of syntactic functions. Traditionally, subject and object are primitive units of syntactic analysis, but Croft argues that syntactic functions are derived from constructions with similar arguments. On this account, subject and object are emergent categories that represent generalizations over similar referring terms in different argument-structure constructions. Following Croft (2001: 56), we can represent the category of subject (in English) in a taxonomy of construction-specific syntactic functions that abstracts away from construction- and verb-specific properties at higher levels of syntactic representation (71).

(71)

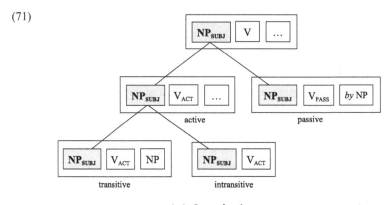

4.4 Conclusion

In this section, we have considered construction-based accounts of three basic syntactic categories: word classes, phrasal constituents, and grammatical relations or syntactic functions. All three categories can be analyzed as emergent concepts that arise from language users' experience with particular lexemes and constructions. More specifically, we have seen that syntactic categories can be defined as networks including the same types of associations as constructions:

• Word classes are defined by filler-slot associations that combine individual lexemes with particular word-class schemas.
• Phrasal constituents involve the full range of associative relations that have been proposed for the analysis of constructions.
• And syntactic functions are represented in taxonomic networks that generalize over similar types of arguments in different argument-structure constructions.

The network approach to syntactic categories presents a radical alternative to the traditional "toolkit approach" in which word classes, phrasal constituents, and syntactic functions are defined as primitive categories that linguists use as "tools" for syntax analysis (Jackendoff 2002a: 75). In the network approach, syntactic categories are not tools or primitive concepts but emergent categories that arise from language use.

The emergentist view of syntactic categories raises new questions for the study of language acquisition and language change. There is a large body of research on the acquisition of grammatical constructions (Lieven et al. 2003; Diessel 2004; Abbott-Smith and Behrens 2006; Goldberg 2006; Höder 2012) and constructional change (Bergs and Diewald 2008; Hilpert 2013, 2021; Traugott and Trausdale 2013; Van de Velde 2014; Coussé et al. 2018; Zehneter 2019; Sommerer and Smirnova 2020). However, syntactic categories are only rarely considered in construction-based research on L1 acquisition and language change. One reason for this might be that the traditional conception of syntactic categories as primitive concepts is inconsistent with the emergentist view of linguistic structure in the usage-based approach. However, if we redefine syntactic categories in terms of networks, they become an integral part of the constructicon and an important topic for usage-based research on acquisition and change.

5 The Global Network: Paradigms, Families, and Neighborhoods

Having analyzed syntactic categories and constructions, this final section is concerned with the global organization of the constructicon. There is general consensus among usage-based scholars that constructions are interrelated. In an oft-cited phrase, Langacker (1991: 263) described grammar as a "structured inventory of conventional linguistic units," suggesting that the constructicon is not just a repository of isolated constructions but has internal structure. In generative grammar, syntactic structures are related by transformations or syntactic derivations. However, since construction grammar has abandoned syntactic derivations, there has been a tendency to analyze constructions in isolation. Following Goldberg (2006: 25), it is commonly assumed that every structural pattern "is best analyzed on its own terms, without relying on explicit reference to possible alternative phrases." There are good reasons to eliminate syntactic derivations, but a number of recent studies have argued that constructions are not isolated entities but combined to particular configurations of symbolic units by horizontal relations (Cappelle 2006; Booij 2010; Van de Velde 2014; Diessel 2015; 2019a; Perek 2015; Fonteyn and Van de Pol 2016; Booij and Audring 2017; Lyngfelt et al. 2018; Norde and Morris 2018; Audring 2019; Diewald 2020; Jackendoff and Audring 2020; Lorenz 2020; Sommerer and Smirnova 2020; Smirnova 2021; Ungerer 2021; Hoffmann 2022; Sommerer 2022).

Horizontal relations have become a central topic of research in construction grammar in recent years, but the phenomena analyzed in terms of horizontal relations are diverse, ranging from inflectional paradigms in morphology to general word order patterns in syntax. On the face of it, these phenomena seem to have little in common; but in the following, I argue that horizontal relations describe particular types of associations that are consistently motivated by two related concepts of gestalt perception: similarity and contrast.

5.1 Why the Constructicon Needs Horizontal Relations

Horizontal relations have been described by different names. Apart from the term "horizontal relations," which has been used in many studies, some researchers have used the notions of sister relations (Audring 2019), paradigmatic relations (Diewald and Politt 2022), and lateral relations (Diessel 2019a) as alternative names.

In a first step, we can define horizontal relations as relations that combine two or more constructions at the same level of specificity. There is a close connection between the taxonomic and horizontal dimensions of grammar. The taxonomic network represents linguistic generalizations in terms of schemas; but since schemas are derived from lower-level constructions with shared properties, one could argue that the taxonomic organization of the constructicon builds on its horizontal dimension.

Let us begin with some examples. In Section 3.5, we saw that Cappelle (2006) proposed a horizontal "relatedness link" to characterize the relationship between the two variants of the English verb-particle construction. Cappelle's analysis concentrates on the schematic representation of the verb-particle construction, but since constructional schemas are derived from lexical strings with similar forms and meanings, it seems reasonable to assume that lexical constructions are also connected by horizontal relations (72).

(72)   [V NP PART] ——— [V PART NP]
             | |
         [take your shoes off] ——— [take off your shoes]

A similar analysis has been proposed for certain types of morphological constructions (Booij 2010; Jackendoff and Audring 2020). For example, Audring (2019) argues that derivational adjectives including the suffixes *-ful* and *-less* constitute a particular pair of constructions that are connected by horizontal relations, which Audring (2019) and Audring and Jackendoff (2020) call "sister relations" (73) (from Audring 2019: 16).

(73)   [N -ful]$_A$ ——— [N -less]$_A$
             | |
         [help$_N$ -ful]$_A$ ——— [help$_N$ -less]$_A$

What led Cappelle, Audring, Jackendoff, and other scholars working in the constructionist paradigm to propose horizontal relations? Audring (2019) argues that horizontal relations are needed to account for constructions that are related in some systematic way but not licensed by a shared schema. For example, N-*ful*$_A$ and N-*less*$_A$ constitute a particular pair of constructions that express a specific semantic contrast (between "having" and "not-having"), but they are not usually analyzed as subtypes of a (specific) higher-level schema. Building on Booij (2010), Audring analyzes the configuration of N-*ful*$_A$ and

N-*less*_A as a **second-order schema** that captures a generalization by a horizontal link rather than a higher-order schema (Jackendoff and Audring 2020).

The proposed analysis of second-order schemas is intriguing, but horizontal links have also been proposed for sister constructions that are taxonomically related to the same mother node. Cappelle's (2006) analysis of the verb-particle construction, for example, includes two horizontally related sub-constructions that are licensed by a higher-order schema with underspecified word order. The horizontal links of second-order schemas are motivated by a missing mother construction; but why should one posit horizontal relations between constructions that are also taxonomically related?

Cappelle (2006) argues that horizontal links are useful to define relations between constructions that complement each other in specific ways. The two sub-constructions of the verb-particle construction, for example, serve particular pragmatic functions in different discourse contexts. Cappelle characterizes the two sub-constructions of the verb-particle construction as **allostructions**, suggesting that they complement each other in the same way as the allomorphs of an abstract morpheme. Like allomorphs, **allostructions** are members of the same category or schema, but since their properties are not immediately predictable from the shared mother node, it seems reasonable to assume that they are also horizontally related.[4]

I agree with Cappelle's claim that horizontal relations are useful to describe constructions in complementary distribution but would add that the main reason for positing horizontal relations is that they are psychologically real. That is, horizontal relations are not (only) needed as a formal device to represent certain types of generalizations; rather, horizontal relations are (also) needed to describe a particular type of association that must not be ignored in a psychologically motivated theory of grammar. These associations are established by two general concepts of gestalt perception, namely by **similarity** and **contrast**.

Similarity and contrast are of central significance to several domain-general processes including categorization, schematization, analogy, and priming that shape horizontal relations. Similarity is a continuous concept that is often difficult to operationalize in empirical studies; yet psychologists agree that the ability to recognize similarity is foundational to human cognition (Gentner 1983). Note that the notions of similarity and contrast entail each other. If two or more elements are similar, they also form a contrast as they are perceived as distinct entities. And, conversely, if two or more elements are contrastive, they are also similar to each other, as the perception of contrast presupposes that the elements in question have some properties in

---

[4] Audring (2019) and Hoffmann (2020) argue that the analysis of allostructions does not need taxonomic relations (in addition to horizontal relations).

common. Similarity and contrast should thus be seen as poles of a continuum rather than as separate concepts.

This continuum provides the conceptual foundation for the analysis of horizontal relations. At one end of the continuum, horizontal links combine constructions that have some salient properties in common; and at the other end of the continuum, they combine constructions that form some kind of contrast or opposition (Diessel 2019a: 197–248). In between the two poles, horizontal links combine constructions that exhibit aspects of both similarity and contrast; but at the poles of the continuum, there is a clear difference between relations of similarity and relations of contrast. The two types of horizontal relations define two general phenomena of grammar that are crucial to the global organization of the constructicon: Horizontal relations of similarity define construction families (and neighborhoods); and horizontal relations of contrast define grammatical paradigms. In the remainder of this section, I describe the three phenomena in turn, beginning with paradigms.

5.2 Paradigms

The notion of paradigm is primarily used in morphology, but in this Element, I use the notion of paradigm in a broader sense subsuming both morphological and syntactic constructions that form a contrast or opposition.

5.2.1 Morphological Paradigms

Morphological paradigms are commonly used to describe inflected word forms. Minimally, a paradigm consists of two related forms (e.g. singular vs. plural); but inflectional paradigms can also comprise a large number of category members. English does not have much inflectional morphology, but other languages have complex paradigms that are defined by several inflectional categories. Traditionally, inflectional paradigms are represented in cross-tables, as the one in (74), which shows a partial paradigm of noun inflection in Even (a Tungusic language spoken in Siberia) that is defined by two categories, that is, case and number.

(74)   Even *ǰuu* 'house' (Malchukov 1995: 9)

	SG	PL
NOM	*ǰuu*	*ǰuu-l*
ACC	*ǰuu-w*	*ǰuu-l-w*
DAT	. . .	. . .

Disregarding irregular forms (e.g. suppletion), inflected word forms are usually derived from a lexical stem and a set of inflectional affixes that are linked together by concatenating rules. However, in construction morphology, inflected words are not derived from separate morphemes but licensed by an inflectional schema consisting of an affix and an associated slot for a particular content word (Booij 2010; Jackendoff and Audring 2020). Every inflected form has a particular semantic value that is determined by its relationship to other word forms in the paradigm, which together constitute a system that Diewald (2020) and others have characterized as a network (e.g. Diessel 2019a: 18–19, 226–227; Leino 2021; Smirnova 2021; Diewald and Politt 2022).

Like cross-tables, networks are well-suited to define the semantic values of inflected word forms. Yet network models are better suited to model the emergence of morphological paradigms than cross-tables. Cross-tables characterize grammatical paradigms as closed symmetric systems; but, as Bybee (1985) and others have shown, most inflectional paradigms are asymmetrical and organized around a basic member. For example, singular nouns are more basic than plural nouns, and nominative case is more basic than accusative or dative case. There are two reasons why these forms are basic:

- First, they are more frequent than all other category members (Greenberg 1966; Haspelmath and Karjus 2017).
- And second, they are often "structurally unmarked" (Croft 2003) or "zero-coded" (Haspelmath 2021).

Structural **markedness** has been a central topic of cross-linguistic research on grammar since Greenberg (1966). The central finding is that most grammatical paradigms are organized around a basic member that is more frequent and less explicitly marked than all other category members (Croft 2003; Haspelmath 2021). Since the encoding asymmetries of inflectional categories correlate with frequency, it is commonly assumed that markedness is shaped by usage frequency. There is an ongoing debate about the psychological mechanisms behind structural markedness, but many typologists assume that the encoding asymmetries of grammatical paradigms arise from an economic strategy to manipulate frequency-based expectations (Haspelmath and Karjus 2017; Haspelmath 2021; Levshina 2022). To simplify, other things being equal, listeners anticipate the most frequent member of a paradigm; but if, for whatever reason, a less frequent member is used, it may be necessary to signal the occurrence of the less expected member by an extra morpheme. The best example for this strategy is perhaps the alternation between affirmative and negative sentences. Since the vast majority of sentences are non-negative, affirmative sentences are morphologically unmarked, whereas negative sentences are almost always marked by an extra morpheme (75–76) (Miestamo 2005).

(75) a. He is sleeping.
      b. He is **not** sleeping.

(76) a. She is happy.
      b. She is **un**happy.

This strategy of morphological flagging is arguably the driving force behind the emergence of structural markedness, which concerns not only the alternation between affirmative and negative sentences but also inflectional paradigms, such as the paradigm of noun inflection in Even (74), which is typical for case and number marking in languages across the world (Haspelmath 2021). Each inflected word form occurs with a certain frequency that determines its activation value in memory and the likelihood of being selected in usage. Across languages, the most frequent form is nominative singular, which is often formally unmarked or zero-coded (e.g. in Even, Turkish, Malayalam). All other word forms carry at least one affix, and plural nouns in accusative case occur with two affixes, as the schema for plural accusative nouns is the least frequent and least expected category member (Diessel 2019a: 223–248). All of this information is represented in the network in (77).

(77) Partial network of noun inflection in Even

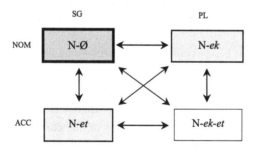

Diewald (2020) argues that paradigms are complex linguistic signs, or "hyper-constructions," that combine certain structural properties with meaning. A **hyper-construction** includes both horizontal links that indicate the contrasts between particular word forms (e.g. singular vs. plural) and vertical links that connect all members of the paradigm to a grammatical category (e.g. the category of number). Diewald's analysis of hyper-constructions is consistent with the nested-network view of the constructicon in which constructional nodes are internally structured as networks (Section 3).

5.2.2 Syntactic Paradigms

Like lexemes, phrases and sentences are organized in paradigms of contrastively related constructions. This is perhaps most evident in the case of inflectional periphrasis. In English, for example, tense and aspect are commonly expressed by periphrastic verb forms that constitute a network of contrastively related constructions (cf. 78), parallel to inflected word forms (cf. 77).

(78)   Partial network of periphrastic verb forms in English

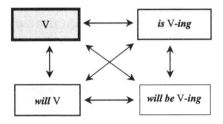

Since inflectional and periphrastic verb forms encode the same categories, it does not come as a surprise that they are organized in parallel fashion; but there are also other types of contrastively related syntactic constructions. For example, all languages have several clause and sentence types to express particular speech act functions and meanings, for example declarative sentences, questions, subordinate clauses, and information-structure constructions such as cleft sentences (König and Siemund 2007). Crucially, while the linguistic encoding of clause and sentence types exhibits a great deal of cross-linguistic variation, there is a general tendency to organize clausal constructions around a basis and unmarked category member. Across languages, we find that declarative main clauses are formally unmarked compared to questions, subordinate clauses, and information-structure constructions (König and Siemund 2007). Consider, for example, the following sentences from English and French.

(79)

	ENGLISH	FRENCH
DECL. MAIN CL	She saw me	Elle m'a vu
WH QUESTION	**Who did** she see?	**Qui** a-t-elle vu?
YES/NO QUESTION	**Did** she see me?	**Est-ce qu'**elle m'a vu?
ADVERBIAL CL	**If** she saw me	**Si** elle m'a vu …
COMPLEMENT CL	**That** she saw me	**Qu'**elle m'a vu …
RELATIVE CL	The person **who** she saw	La personne **qu'**elle a vue
CLEFT/FOCUS	**It was** me **who** she saw	**C'est** moi **qu'**elle a vu

As can be seen, all of the sentences in (79) include at least one construction-specific grammatical morpheme, except for declarative main clauses, suggesting that main clauses have a particular status in grammar (König and Siemund 2007). They are the basic elements of clause-level constructions, which exhibit the same asymmetries as morphological paradigms. Like the zero-coded forms of morphological inflection, basic declarative main clauses are more frequent and (often) less explicitly marked than other clause and sentence types. Across languages, questions typically include a particular question word or interrogative marker, subordinate clauses include a conjunction, complementizer or relative pronoun, and information-structure constructions are often marked by topic or focus morphemes. Assuming that all of these constructions are defined by their relationship to basic declarative main clauses, we may think of the various clause and sentence types of a language as a network of contrastive constructions, as shown in (80). On this account, questions, subordinate clauses, and information-structure constructions are natural complements of basic main clauses (for related analyses of verb-first and verb-second constructions in German and Dutch, see Diessel 1997 and Van de Velde 2014).

(80)

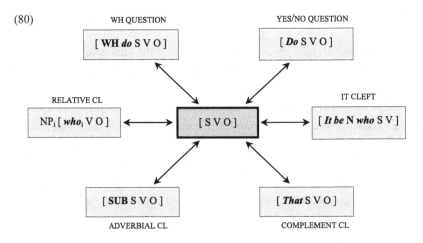

5.2.3 Psycholinguistic Evidence

Psycholinguistic evidence for contrastively related constructions comes from research on linguistic **productivity**. To repeat, in the usage-based approach, linguistic productivity is the likelihood that a constructional schema is extended to new items (Section 3.4). To give a simple example from morphology, if we encounter a new lexeme such as *wug* in an inflectional schema, such as the singular schema of English count nouns (81a), we automatically assume that *wug* is also licensed by the schema for plural nouns (81b) as singular and plural nouns are systematically related (Berko 1958).

(81)	a.	There is a *wug*.
	b.	Now there are two ... *wugs*.

A parallel analysis applies to contrastively related constructions in syntax. For example, if we encounter a novel verb in a declarative main clause, such as *John mooped me*, we automatically assume that *moop* can also be used in questions, subordinate clauses, and other clause and sentence types (e.g. *Did he moop you?*). Both syntactic and morphological constructions are readily extended to new items if they are perceived as natural complements, or paradigmatic alternatives, of a particular category or speech act type.

Experimental evidence for this analysis comes from a study by Perek and Goldberg (2015). Using a language learning paradigm, these researchers taught adult speakers of English an artificial language consisting of six English nouns denoting animals (e.g. *rabbit, monkey*), eight nonce verbs (e.g. *moop, tonk*), and two transitive constructions with different word orders and different functions. One of the two constructions had SOV word order and was exclusively used with full lexical nouns; the other construction had OSV order and occurred with a pronominal object denoting a known or topical referent (82).

(82)   a. The rabbit the monkey mooped.   SOV
        b. Him the rabbit mooped. $O_{PRO}SV$

After training, participants were asked questions to elicit utterances with novel combinations of verbs and constructions (i.e. combinations that did not occur during training). As expected, participants extended the $O_{PRO}SV$ construction to novel verbs if this was motivated by the discourse context, suggesting that the two constructions were used productively if participants conceived of them as opposing terms. However, in a follow-up study, another group of participants learned a language in which both constructions were used with full lexical NPs in the same discourse contexts, suggesting that SOV and OSV occurred in free variation. Crucially, in this case, participants refrained from extending constructions to novel verbs, indicating that the productivity of constructions in experiment 1 was motivated by the fact that participants conceived of SOV and $O_{PRO}SV$ as constructions that complement each other in terms of their pragmatic functions.

5.3 Families and Neighborhoods

Having analyzed grammatical paradigms, let us now turn to construction families and neighborhoods. The terms "family" and "neighborhood" are widely used in psycholinguistics to describe groups of lexical expressions that have same salient properties in common. The shared properties may concern the form or meaning of lexical expressions or both. For example, Schreuder and Baayen (1997) used the term "family" for morphologically complex words including the same lexical stem (e.g. *compute, computer, computable, computerize, computation*), and Luce and Pisoni (1998) used the term "neighborhood" for simple words that differ from each other by only one phoneme or letter (e.g. *rat, cat, sat, bat, at*). The term "family" is also sometimes used to describe groups (or fields) of semantically related expressions (e.g. *farm, field, cow, feed, barn*). There is good evidence in psycholinguistics that formally and/or semantically similar expressions influence each other in language use and acquisition (Vitevitch 2002; Dąbrowska 2008; Gahl et al. 2012); however, the notions of family and neighborhood are not always easy to distinguish. For the purpose of the current discussion, I adopt the following definitions: Both families and neighborhoods describe groups (or pairs) of constructions that have some salient formal and/or semantic properties in common. However, families and neighborhoods are distinguished from each other by taxonomic relations. The term "family" describes a group (or pair) of similar constructions that are categorized as subtypes of the same schema, and the term "neighborhood" describes a group (or pair) of similar constructions that are licensed by different schemas (83).

(83)

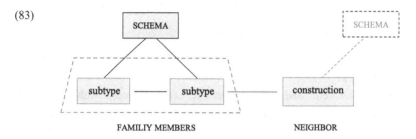

In practice, the distinction between families and neighborhoods is often difficult to make. Similarity is a matter of degree and not all shared properties are represented in schemas that are permanently stored in memory. In what follows, I illustrate the importance of horizontal relations for the overall organization of the constructicon based on two selected examples from English. The proposed analyses should be seen as hypotheses that can be tested with empirical methods in future research.

5.3.1 Argument-Structure Constructions

The prime example of a construction family is the English resultative (Boas 2003; Goldberg and Jackendoff 2004). Resultative constructions vary along several parameters: (i) they can include an adjective or prepositional phrase (84a vs. 84b), (ii) can be transitive or intransitive (84a vs. 84c), and (iii) may select a true argument or "fake object" (84a vs. 84d) (Boas 2003). Considering this variation, Goldberg and Jackendoff (2004: 535) argued that the resultative does not constitute a "unified phenomenon" but "a sort of family of constructions."

(84)   a. John painted the door *red*.
         b. Bill broke the mirror *into pieces*.
         c. The lake froze *rock solid*.
         d. John drank himself *sick*.

The resultative is not an isolated case. In the literature, constructions are commonly described as if they were individual signs; but I would contend that most constructions are organized in families, like the resultative, and that these families are always embedded in a larger neighborhood. Consider, for example, the English verb-particle construction. Cappelle (2006) concentrated on the transitive verb-particle construction (85a–b); but there is also an intransitive verb-particle construction in which the particle appears right after the verb (85c).

(85) a. He took **out** the garbage.
      b. He took the garbage **out**.
      c. He freaked **out**.

Like most other constructions, the verb-particle construction is semantically diverse or polysemous. Jackendoff (2002b) distinguished three semantic subtypes: (i) idiomatic verb-particle constructions in which the meaning of the construction is not directly predictable from the meaning of its parts (86a), (ii) aspectual verb-particle constructions in which the particle serves as an aspectual marker of the verb (86b), and (iii) directional verb-particle constructions in which the particle "satisfies one of the verb's argument positions" as the particle can always be replaced by a directional PP selected by the verb (86c) (Jackendoff 2002b: 75).

(86) a. Turn this **on**.
      b. Finish this **up**.
      c. Put this **down**. ↔ [Put this **on the table**].

Each formal subtype (illustrated in 85a–c) is related to one or more construction neighbors. The intransitive verb-particle construction is very similar to constructions including an unaccusative verb and a directional adverb or resultative adjective. These constructions have essentially the same form and meaning, except that the final element of the unaccusative construction is not a particle (87a) but either an adverb (87b) or adjective (87c) (according to Bolinger 1971).

(87) a. The bottle fell **down**.   PART
      b. The man went **outside**.   ADV
      c. The door broke **open**.   ADJ

The transitive verb-particle construction also has several construction neighbors. First, if the particle precedes the object, the construction has the same surface form as an intransitive sentence in which the verb is followed by a prepositional phrase (88a–b). Of course, unlike particles, prepositions cannot occur after the associated NP (89a–b); but if the particle precedes the direct object, the two grammatical patterns are strikingly similar to each other. As Huddleston and Pullum (2002: 282) pointed out, a VP such as *turn in NP* is ambiguous between the transitive verb-particle construction (90a) and an intransitive construction in which *in* serves as preposition of a locational adjunct (90b).

| (88) | a. He took **off** the label. | V-PART-NP |
| | b. He jumped **off** the wall. | V-P-NP |

| (89) | a. He took the label **off**. | V-NP-PART |
| | b. *He jumped the wall **off**. | V-NP-P |

| (90) | a. He turned **in** the prisoner. | V-PART-NP |
| | b. He turned **in** the wrong direction. | V-PP |

Another group of constructions that resemble the two subtypes of the transitive verb-particle construction are causative sentences including certain types of adjectives, participles, or infinitives, which may precede or follow the object like a particle, as illustrated by the examples in (91a–b) to (93a–b) (from Bolinger 1971: 71–81).

| (91) | a. He held the door **open**. | ADJ |
| | b. He held **open** the door. | |

| (92) | a. He made the facts **known**. | PTC |
| | b. He made **known** the facts. | |

| (93) | a. He let the lines **go**. | INF |
| | b. He let **go** the lines. | |

Finally, the so-called "time-*away* construction" is similar to the transitive verb-particle construction, as *away* can precede or follow the time NP (94a–b). However, in contrast to a transitive sentence such as *He put the weapon away*, the verb of the time-*away* construction does not subcategorize the postverbal NP as an argument, according to Jackendoff (1997).

| (94) | a. He slept the afternoon **away**. |
| | b. He slept **away** the afternoon. |

Generalizing across these observations, we may characterize the verb-particle construction as a construction family with several syntactic neighbors that share some salient semantic and formal properties with individual family members (95). Importantly, while one might argue that the three basic subtypes of the verb-particle construction are licensed by a shared schema, it seems unlikely that grammar includes permanently stored schemas of individual family members and their specific neighbors.

(95)

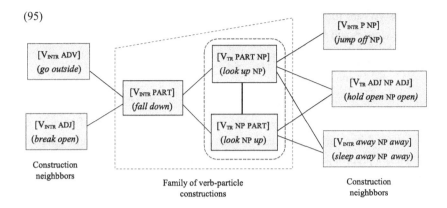

Construction
neighbbors

Family of verb-particle
constructions

Construction
neighbbors

5.3.2 Copular Clauses

Like argument-structure constructions, copular clauses constitute a construction family with several syntactic neighbors (Petré 2014). In English, copular clauses are formed by combining a copular verb, notably *be*, with a complement, which may be an adjective (96a), nominal (96b), or prepositional phrase (96c).

(96)   a. He is sick.
       b. He is a friend.
       c. He is in London.

Each structural type is used with a variety of meanings. For example, copular clauses including a predicate adjective may express a permanent property or temporary state (97a–b), and copular clauses including a predicate nominal may express identity (97c), membership (97d), possession (97e), or existence (97f).

(97)   a. She is tall.
       b. She is sick.
       c. That's me.
       d. This is a noun.
       e. That is mine.
       f. There is no problem.

The various types of copular clauses are horizontally related to different construction neighbors. For example, copular clauses including a predicate adjective are related to passive constructions including the auxiliary *be* and a past participle. While the *be*-passive can designate an action (*The rabbit was chased by the fox*), it is also often used to describe a resultant state (98b), similar to a (predicate) adjective (98a). In addition, *be* can serve as an auxiliary of the progressive (98c), but the semantic relationship between copular clauses and progressive verb forms is (semantically) much more remote than that between copular clauses and stative passives.

(98)   a. The door is open.
         b. The door is opened.
         c. The door is opening.

Copular clauses including a predicate nominal are reminiscent of transitive clauses including verbs of possession such as *have* (99a–b); and copular clauses including a prepositional phrase are both semantically and structurally similar to intransitive clauses including a posture verb and a locational adjunct (100a–b).

(99)   a. He is a friend.
         b. He has a friend.

(100)   a. He is behind this wall.
         b. He stands behind this wall.

The graph in (101) seeks to capture the essence of the previous analysis in the form of a network in which the three main structural types of copular clauses are grouped together to a construction family with individual family members being linked to different construction neighbors.

(101)

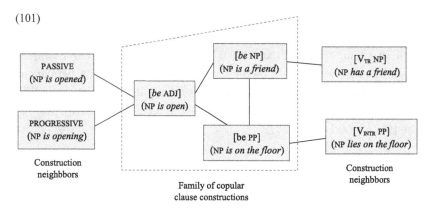

Construction families and neighborhoods are key to characterize the global organization of the constructicon, but horizontal relations have also been proposed for more local phenomena such as "constructional contamination" (Pijpops and Van de Velde 2016).

5.3.3 Constructional Contamination

The term "constructional contamination" was coined by Pijpops and Van de Velde (2016) in order to describe how two (or more) alternating sub-constructions of the same schema are influenced by lexical frequencies of a construction neighbor. Pijpops and Van de Velde (2016) and Pijpops et al. (2018) present several case studies of constructional contamination in Dutch; but here we consider a case study from English by Hilpert and Flach (2022). English has fairly rigid word order, but there is one category that is often very flexible in its distribution, that is, the category of adverb. However, the flexibility of adverb placement is contingent on the construction. In passive constructions, for example, adverbs can precede or follow the main verb (or participle) they modify (102a–b).

(102) a. Garlic is **widely believed** to help protect against infections.
       b. Garlic is **believed widely** to help protect against infections.

The two ordering patterns are not fully equivalent in terms of their meaning, but they are similar enough to analyze them as sub-constructions of the same schema (parallel to the analysis Cappelle proposed for the two sub-constructions of the verb-particle construction). What Hilpert and Flach observed in their study is that the order of adverb and verb in passive constructions is contaminated by the order of adverb and participle in complex NPs in which the adverb is generally preposed to the participle (103a–b).

(103) a. **widely believed** myth
       b. * a **believed widely** myth

Using data from a large corpus, Hilpert and Flach showed that passive constructions tend to occur with the order adverb-participle if they include a lexical string such as *widely believed* that is frequent in complex NPs. Combinations of adverb and participle that are rare or absent in complex NPs often occur with the order participle-adverb in passive constructions, suggesting that complex NPs including a participle and adverb influence, or contaminate, the word order alternation in passive sentences, which Hilpert and Flach interpret as evidence for a horizontal link between these constructions (104).

(104)

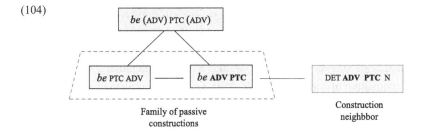

Family of passive
constructions

Construction
neighbbor

5.3.4 Psycholinguistic Evidence

Good evidence for construction families and neighborhoods comes from research on structural priming (Diessel 2019a: 202–205; Ungerer 2021). Linguistic expressions that are similar in form and meaning prime each other. This holds for both lexical expressions and constructions. A lexical item such as *tree*, for example, facilitates the activation of semantically or formally related expressions such as *wood* and *bee* (Dell 1986). Parallel priming effects occur with grammatical constructions. For example, a number of studies have shown that speakers' choice between alternating argument-structure constructions, such as the two constructions of the dative alternation (e.g. *He gave John the book* vs. *He gave the book to John*) or the two word order patterns of the transitive verb-particle construction (e.g. *He turned the music on* vs. *He turned on the music*), are crucially facilitated if a language user has experienced the same (sub-)construction in the previous discourse (Bock 1986; Gries 2005). If prime source and prime target are identical, psycholinguists speak of repetition priming (Pickering and Ferreira 2008). However, structural priming also affects distinct but similar constructions. For example, Bock and Loebell (1990) observed that active sentences including a locative *by*-phrase (e.g. *The 747 was landing by the airport's tower*) prime passive sentences including an agentive *by*-phrase (e.g. *The 747 was alerted by the airport's tower*); and Hare and Goldberg (2000) showed that a sentence such as *They provided us with a meal* primes a structurally distinct but semantically related sentence such as *They offered us a meal*. In general, there is a large body of research indicating that structural priming is an important determinant for selecting a particular construction in both production and comprehension (for a review, see Pickering and Ferreira 2008). Since the effect is not restricted to repetition priming, it seems reasonable to assume that similar constructions are horizontally related even if these constructions are not licensed by the same schema or mother node (Ungerer 2021).

A second piece of evidence for horizontal relations comes from research on language acquisition and change. There is increasing evidence that the development of a construction in L1 acquisition is often influenced by construction neighbors. For example, Abbott-Smith and Behrens (2006) found that the acquisition of stative passives in German (105a) is facilitated by children's prior acquisition of copular clauses (105b), which they explain by the similarity between copular clauses and stative passives. Both constructions include an inflected form of the verb *sein* 'be', designate a resultant state, and have the same word order. Since children learn copular clauses with *sein* very early, they have fewer difficulties with stative passives, formed with *sein*, than with event passives, formed with *werden* 'become' (105c).

(105) a. *Das Fenster ist geöffnet.*
The window is opened.PTC
'The window is opened.'

b. *Das Fenster ist offen.*
The window is open.ADJ
'The window is open.'

c. *Das Fenster wird geöffnet.*
The window is.being opened.PTC
'The window is being opened.'

Similar neighborhood effects have been observed in research on constructional change (Van de Velde 2014; Fonteyn and Van de Pol 2016; de Smet et al. 2018; Sommerer and Smirnova 2020). For example, Bloom (2021) argued that the increasing predominance of SVO word order in Middle English main clauses had an impact on word order in relative clauses. In Old English, the verb typically occurred at the end of a relative clause (106a). However, in Middle English, there was a growing tendency to place long and indefinite objects after the verb in subject relatives, especially when the relative clause was introduced by a relative pronoun that could also be used as a demonstrative pronoun in main clauses (106b). Initially, the word order change was motivated by the oft-noted preference for using long and indefinite constituents at the end of a clause. Yet Bloom argued that the development was reinforced by SVO word order in main clauses, as the change from OV to VO was particularly advanced in subject relatives that resembled main clauses (i.e. subject relatives that were introduced by a demonstrative relative marker rather than the older relative particle *þe*, which did not occur in main clauses).

(106) Subject relatives in Old and Middle English (from Bloom 2021: 1)

a. *Se munuc [þe þæt hordern heold]*RC ...
the monk REL.PART the treasury.ACC kept
'The monk, who kept the treasury ....'

b. *A man [that drynket hony]*RC ...
a man REL.PRO drinks honey
'A man who drinks honey ....'

Note that object relatives were not affected by the described word order change as object relatives do not include an overt object. Like Old English, Modern English has object relatives that express the patient before the agent in the head of the relative clause (107), so that the order of semantic roles in object relatives is markedly distinct from that in main clauses, which arguably explains why object relatives cause more difficulties in L1 acquisition (Diessel and Tomasello 2005) and processing (Wells et al. 2009) than subject relatives.

(107)   [The house]$_{PA}$ [[they]$_{AG}$ built]$_{RC}$ was expensive.

5.4 Conclusion

In conclusion, a number of recent studies have argued that a psychologically plausible model of the constructicon includes horizontal relations between constructions at the same abstraction level. Elaborating on this claim, this final section has argued that a person's knowledge of grammar involves pairs or groups of horizontally related constructions that can be divided into two (or three) basic types: (i) grammatical paradigms and (ii) construction families (and neighborhoods). The distinction between paradigms and families (and neighborhoods) is based on the following criteria.

First, construction families and neighborhoods are based on similarity relations, whereas grammatical paradigms are based on relationships of contrast. Second, families and paradigms are organized in different network systems. Construction families are open-ended groups of similar constructions with fluid boundaries to neighboring constructions, whereas grammatical paradigms are based on pairs or sets of complementary constructions that form a (fairly) closed system of mutually exclusive expressions. And finally, construction families and paradigms are morphologically distinguished. Construction families are characterized by overlapping properties of form and meaning that are not specifically marked, whereas grammatical paradigms are usually organized around a basic category member that is zero-coded or morphologically unmarked. Table 6 summarizes the main points of the previous discussion.

Evidence for horizontal relations comes from research on priming, productivity, L1 acquisition, and constructional change. Constructions that are

Table 6 Construction families and paradigms

	FAMILIES	PARADIGMS
Horizontal relations are perceived as being . . .	similar	contrastive
The system of horizontally related constructions is . . .	open-ended	closed
The encoding of constructions involves . . .	no particular marking	an opposition between overt and zero marking

organized in families and neighborhoods reinforce each other in usage and development; and constructions that are organized in paradigms can be extended to novel lexical expressions. Put differently, construction families help to explain how structural priming and family size affect the activation and development of constructions (in acquisition and change), and grammatical paradigms are key to explaining linguistic productivity.

On a final note, let me reiterate that families and paradigms form a continuum with no clear-cut boundary between them. The previous discussion has concentrated on grammatical patterns that are perceived as being similar or contrastive. However, given that similarity and contrast are always simultaneously present, it does not come as a surprise that many constructions exhibit properties of both families and paradigms. A good example are allostructions such as the two variants of the (transitive) verb-particle construction (see Section 5.3.1) or the two variants of the dative alternation (108a–b).

(108)   a. He gave John the book.
        b. He gave the book to John.

Alternating constructions of this type have been studied intensively in recent years (e.g. Gries 2003; Stefanowitsch and Gries 2003; Gries et al. 2005; Bresnan et al. 2007; Iwata 2008; Cornille and Delbecque 2008; Hoffmann 2011; Wolk et al. 2013; Perek 2015). There is abundant evidence that speakers' choice between one or the other construction correlates with semantic, pragmatic, and structural features (e.g. length), indicating that allostructions are perceived as opposing terms. However, in contrast to the constructions of a grammatical paradigm (e.g. singular vs. plural nouns), allostructions are not mutually exclusive. There is an area of functional overlap where speakers can freely choose between them, suggesting allostructions are connected by horizontal associations of similarity and contrast alike.

6 Concluding Remarks

Since the advance of construction grammar more than thirty years ago, the constructicon has been a key concept of the constructivist approach; but it is only recently that researchers have begun to investigate the cognitive organization of the constructicon in some detail. The inheritance model of classical construction grammar was inspired by computer science and has been mainly concerned with the taxonomic dimension of grammar. However, while grammar includes an important taxonomic dimension, there is growing consensus among usage-based scholars that a psychologically plausible theory of grammar involves more than a taxonomy of hierarchically related constructions. Combining research from linguistics with research in psychology, usage-based linguists have expanded the inheritance model of classical construction grammar into a multidimensional network approach in which all aspects of a person's linguistic knowledge are analyzed in terms of associations. Associations originate from experience and are in principle always changing under the influence of domain-general processes of language use. The inheritance links of classical construction grammar correspond to taxonomic associations; but in addition, grammar includes several other kinds of links or associations. In this Element, we have considered five different types of associative relations to characterize a person's knowledge of grammar:

  (i) symbolic relations, which combine form and meaning,
 (ii) sequential relations, which combine linguistic elements in linear order,
(iii) taxonomic relations, which combine constructional schemas with lexical constructions or constructions at different levels of abstraction,
(iv) filler-slot relations, which combine the slots of constructional schemas with particular lexical and phrasal fillers, and
 (v) horizontal relations, which combine constructions of the same abstraction level to paradigms, families, and neighborhoods.

Each relation is shaped by particular cognitive processes and characterized by specific properties. Symbolic relations, for example, are usually established by processes of social cognition (or theory-of-mind), whereas taxonomic relations are usually created by abstraction (or schematization). Some of these relations can be divided into more specific types. Horizontal relations, for example, may be divided into relations of similarity and relations of contrast, and symbolic relations may be divided into associations between lexical concepts that are related to world knowledge and associations between abstract semantic concepts that define the meanings of constructional schemas.

There may be other types of associative relations and alternative ways of analyzing the five associations considered in this Element. The multidimensional network approach is not yet a fully developed theory and there are many theoretical and empirical desiderata. What is needed is more theoretical research to (re-)define grammatical concepts in terms of networks and to formulate more precise hypotheses as to how these networks emerge, stabilize, and change. The network conception of the constructicon draws on a large body of extant research, but as of now few studies have been designed to examine specific predictions of the network approach. What is needed is more corpus research to investigate the statistical properties of grammar; more experimental research to test specific hypotheses as to how constructions, categories, and lexemes influence each other in usage, acquisition, and change; and more computational research to simulate the emergence of linguistic structure and meaning. The multidimensional network approach casts a fresh light on many linguistic phenomena, but the approach is still in its infancy and needs to be elaborated in much more detail in future research.

Abbreviations

ACC	accusative
ACT	active
A/ADJ	adjective
ADV	adverb
AG	agent
AUX	auxiliary
C	consonant
CC	complement clause
CL	clause
CONJ	conjunction
COP	copula
DAT	dative
DET	determiner
ERG	ergative
G/GEN	genitive
INF	infinitive
INTR	intransitive
N	noun
NML	nominalizer
NOM	nominative
NP	noun phrase
OBJ	object
OV	object-verb order
P	adposition
PA	patient
PART	particle
PASS	passive
PL	plural
POSS	possessive marker
PP	adpositional phrase
PRO	pronoun
PST	past tense
PTC	participle
REL.PART	relative particle
REL.PRO	relative pronoun
REL/RC	relative clause

S	sentence/clause
SG	singular
SUB	subordinate conjunction
SUBJ	subject
SVO	subject-verb-object
TR	transitive
V	verb
V	vowel
VO	verb-object order
VP	verb phrase
WH	question word
X(P)	any (phrasal) category

References

Abbot-Smith, K. and Behrens, H. (2006). How known constructions influence the acquisition of other constructions: The German passive and future constructions. *Cognitive Science* 30, 995–1026.

Abbot-Smith, K. and Tomasello, M. (2006). Exemplar-learning and schematization in a usage-based account of syntactic acquisition. *The Linguistic Review* 23, 275–290.

Aitchison, J. (2012). *Words in the Mind: An Introduction to the Mental Lexicon* (6th ed.). Oxford: Basil Blackwell.

Altmann, G. T. M. and Kamide, Y. (1999). Incremental interpretation at verbs: Restricting the domain of subsequent reference. *Cognition* 73, 247–264.

Altmann, G. T. M. and Mirković, J. (2009). Incrementality and prediction in human sentence processing. *Cognitive Science* 33, 583–609.

Anderson, J. R. (2005). *Cognitive Psychology and Its Implications* (6th ed.). New York: Worth Publishers.

Audring, J. (2019). Mothers or sisters? The encoding of morphological knowledge. *Word Structure* 12, 274–296.

Barðdal, J. (2006). Construction-specific properties of syntactic subjects in Icelandic and German. *Cognitive Linguistics* 17, 39–106.

Barth, D. and Kapatsinski, V. (2017). A multimodel inference approach to categorical variant choice: Construction, priming and frequency effects on the choice between full and contracted forms of *am*, *are* and *is*. *Corpus Linguistics and Linguistic Theory* 13, 1–58.

Bates, E. and MacWhinney, B. (1989). Functionalism and the competition model. In B. MacWhinney and E. Bates (eds.), *The Crosslinguistic Study of Sentence Processing*, 3–73. Cambridge: Cambridge University Press.

Behrens, H. (2009). Usage-based and emergentist approaches to language acquisition. *Linguistics* 47, 383–411.

Bergs, A. and Diewald, G. (eds.) (2008). *Constructions and Language Change*. Berlin: Mouton de Gruyter.

Berko, J. (1958). The child's learning of English morphology. *Word* 14, 150–177.

Biber, D., Johansson, S., Leech, G., Conrad, S., and Finegan, E. (1999). *Longman Grammar of Spoken and Written English*. Harlow: Pearson Education.

Bickel, B. (2011). Grammatical relations typology. In J. J. Song (ed.), *The Oxford Handbook of Linguistic Typology*, 399–444. Oxford: Oxford University Press.

Bloom, B. (2021). Lateral relations and multiple source constructions: The Old English subject relative clause and the Norwegian *han-mannen*-construction. PhD dissertation, Friedrich Schiller University Jena.

Boas, H. C. (2003). *A Constructional Approach to Resultatives*. Stanford, CA: Center for the Study of Language and Information (CSLI).

Boas, H. C. (2010). The syntax–lexicon continuum in construction grammar: A case study of English communication verbs. *Belgian Journal of Linguistics* 24, 54–82.

Boas, H. C. (2013). Cognitive construction grammar. In T. Hoffmann and G. Trousdale (eds.), *The Oxford Handbook of Construction Grammar*, 233–252. Oxford: Oxford University Press.

Boas, H. C. (2017). Computational resources: FrameNet and constructicon. In B. Dancygier (ed.), *The Cambridge Handbook of Cognitive Linguistics*, 549–573. Cambridge: Cambridge University Press.

Bock, K. (1986). Syntactic persistence in language production. *Cognitive Psychology* 18, 355–387.

Bock, K. and Loebell, H. (1990). Framing sentences. *Cognition* 35, 1–39.

Bolinger, D. (1971). *The Phrasal Verb in English*. Cambridge, MA: Harvard University Press.

Booij, G. (2010). *Construction Morphology*. Oxford: Oxford University Press.

Booij, G. and Audring, J. (2017). Construction morphology and the parallel architecture of grammar. *Cognitive Science* 41, 277–302.

Bouso, T. (2020). The growth of the transitivising reaction object construction. *Constructions and Frames* 12, 239–271.

Bower, G. H. (2000). A brief history of memory research. In E. Tulving and F. I. M. Craik (eds.), *The Oxford Handbook of Memory*, 3–32. Oxford: Oxford University Press.

Braine, M. D. S. (1976). Children's first word combinations. *Monographs of the Society for Research in Child Development* 41.

Bresnan, J., Cueni, A., Nikitina, T., and Baayen, H. R. (2007). Predicting the dative alternation. In G. Boume, I. Kraemer, and J. Zwarts (eds.), *Cognitive Foundations of Interpretation*, 69–94. Amsterdam: Royal Netherlands Academy of Science.

Bresnan, J. and Ford, M. (2010). Predicting syntax: Processing dative constructions in American and Australian varieties of English. *Language* 86, 186–213.

Bresnan, J. and Hay, J. (2008). Gradient grammar: An effect of animacy on the syntax of *give* in New Zealand and American English. *Lingua* 118, 245–259.

Buchanan, M. (2002). *Nexus: Small Worlds and the Groundbreaking Science of Networks*. New York: W. W. Norton & Company.

Bybee, J. (1985). *Morphology: A Study on the Relation between Meaning and Form*. Amsterdam: John Benjamins.

Bybee, J. (1995). Regular morphology and the lexicon. *Language and Cognitive Processes* 10, 425–455.

Bybee, J. (2001). *Phonology and Language Use*. Cambridge: Cambridge University Press.

Bybee, J. (2006). From usage to grammar: The mind's response to repetition. *Language* 82, 711–733.

Bybee, J. (2007). *Frequency of Use and the Organization of Language*. Cambridge: Cambridge University Press.

Bybee, J. (2010). *Language, Cognition, and Usage*. Cambridge: Cambridge University Press.

Bybee, J. and Beckner, C. (2010). Usage-based theory. In B. Heine and H. Narrog (eds.), *The Oxford Handbook of Linguistic Analysis*, 827–855. Oxford: Oxford University Press.

Bybee, J. and Hopper. P. (eds.) (2001). *Frequency and the Emergence of Linguistic Structure*. Amsterdam: John Benjamins.

Bybee, J. and Moder, C. L. (1983). Morphological classes as natural categories. *Language* 59, 251–270.

Bybee, J. and Scheibman, J. (1999). The effect of usage on degrees of constituency: The reduction of *don't* in English. *Linguistics* 37, 575–596.

Bybee, J. and Thompson, S. A. (2022). Interaction and grammar: Predicative adjectives in English conversation. *Languages* 7, 2.

Cappelle, B. (2006). Particle placement and the case for "allostructions." *Constructions* 1, 1–28.

Chafe, W. (1994). *Discourse, Consciousness, and Time: The Flow and Displacement of Conscious Experience in Speaking and Writing*. Chicago, IL: University of Chicago Press.

Chomsky, N. (1965). *Aspects of a Theory of Syntax*. Cambridge, MA: MIT Press.

Chomsky, N. (1995). *The Minimalist Program*. Cambridge, MA: MIT Press.

Colleman, T. and de Clerck, B. (2011). Constructional semantics on the move: On semantic specialization in the English double-object construction. *Cognitive Linguistics* 22, 183–209.

Collins, A. M. and Loftus, E. F. (1975). A spreading-activation theory of semantic processing. *Psychological Review* 82, 407–428.

Cornille, B. and Delbecque, N. (2008). Speaker commitment: Back to the speaker. Evidence from Spanish alternations. *Belgian Journal of Linguistics* 22, 37–62.

Coussé, E., Andersson, P., and Olofsson, J. (eds.) (2018). *Grammaticalization Meets Construction Grammar*. Amsterdam: John Benjamins.

Croft, W. (1991). *Syntactic Categories and Grammatical Relations: The Cognitive Organization of Information*. Chicago, IL: Chicago University Press.

Croft, W. (2001). *Radical Construction Grammar*. Oxford: Oxford University Press.

Croft, W. (2003). *Typology and Universals* (2nd ed.). Cambridge: Cambridge University Press.

Culbertson, J., Smolensky. P., and Legendre, G. (2012). Learning biases predict a word order universal. *Cognition* 122, 306–329.

Dąbrowska, E. (2008). The effects of frequency and neighbourhood density on adult speakers' productivity with Polish case inflections: An empirical test of usage-based approaches to morphology. *Journal of Memory and Language* 58, 931–951.

Dąbrowska, E. and Lieven, E. V. M. (2005). Towards a lexically specific grammar of children's question constructions. *Cognitive Linguistics* 16, 437–474.

Dell, G. S. (1986). A spreading-activation theory of retrieval in sentence production. *Psychological Review* 93, 283–321.

De Smet, H., D'hoedt, F., Fonteyn, L., and Van Goethem, K. (2018). The changing functions of competing forms: Attraction and differentiation. *Cognitive Linguistics* 29, 197–234.

Diessel, H. (1997). Verb-first constructions in German. In M. Verspoor, L. K. Dong, and E. Sweetser (eds.), *Lexical and Syntactical Constructions and the Construction of Meaning*, 51–68. Amsterdam: John Benjamins.

Diessel, H. (2004). *The Acquisition of Complex Sentences*. Cambridge: Cambridge University Press.

Diessel, H. (2007). Frequency effects in language acquisition, language use, and diachronic change. *New Ideas in Psychology* 25, 108–127.

Diessel, H. (2013). Construction grammar and first language acquisition. In T. Hoffmann and G. Trousdale (eds.), *The Oxford Handbook of Construction Grammar*, 347–364. Oxford: Oxford University Press.

Diessel, H. (2015). Usage-based construction grammar. In E. Dąbrowska and D. Divjak (eds.), *Handbook of Cognitive Linguistics*, 295–321. Berlin: Mouton de Gruyter.

Diessel, H. (2016). Frequency and lexical specificity. A critical review. In H. Behrens and S. Pfänder (eds.), *Experience Counts: Frequency Effects in Language*, 209–237. Berlin: Mouton de Gruyter.

Diessel, H. (2017). Usage-based linguistics. In M. Aronoff (ed.), *Oxford Research Encyclopedia of Linguistics*. New York: Oxford University Press.

Diessel, H. (2019a). *The Grammar Network: How Linguistic Structure Is Shaped by Language Use.* Cambridge: Cambridge University Press.

Diessel, H. (2019b). Preposed adverbial clauses: Functional adaptation and diachronic inheritance. In K. Schmidtke-Bode, N. Levshina, S. Michaelis, and I. A. Seržant (eds.), *Explanation in Linguistic Typology: Diachronic Sources, Functional Motivations and the Nature of the Evidence*, 191–226. Leipzig: Language Science Press.

Diessel, H. (2020). A dynamic network approach to the study of syntax. *Frontiers in Psychology* 11. https://doi.org/10.3389/fpsyg.2020.604853.

Diessel, H. and Hilpert, M. (2016). Frequency effects in grammar. In M. Aronoff (ed.), *Oxford Research Encyclopedia of Linguistics.* New York: Oxford University Press. https://doi.org/10.1093/acrefore/9780199384655.013.120.

Diessel, H. and Tomasello, M. (2005). A new look at the acquisition of relative clauses. *Language* 81, 1–25.

Diewald, G. (2020). Paradigms lost – paradigms regained: Paradigms as hyper-constructions. In L. Sommerer and E. Smirnova (eds.), *Nodes and Networks in Diachronic Construction Grammar*, 277–316. Amsterdam: John Benjamins.

Diewald, G. and Politt, K. (2022). *Paradigms Regained: Theoretical and Empirical Arguments for the Assessment of the Notion of Paradigm.* Leipzig: Language Science Press.

Divjak, D. (2019). *Frequency in Language: Memory, Attention and Learning.* Oxford: Oxford University Press.

Dixon, R. M. W. (1994). *Ergativity.* Cambridge: Cambridge University Press.

Dryer, M. S. (1988). Object-article order and adjective-noun order: Dispelling a myth. *Lingua* 74, 185–217.

Dryer, M. S. (1992). The Greenbergian word order correlations. *Language* 68, 81–138.

Dryer, M. S. (2019). Grammaticalization accounts of word order correlations. In K. Schmidtke-Bode, N. Levshina, S. Michaelis, and I. A. Seržant (eds.), *Explanation in Linguistic Typology: Diachronic Sources, Functional Motivations and the Nature of the Evidence*, 763–796. Leipzig: Language Science Press.

Dryer, M. S. and Haspelmath, M. (eds.), (2013). *The World Atlas of Language Structures.* Oxford: Oxford University Press.

Elman, J. L., Bates, E. A., Johnson, M. H. et al. (1996). *Rethinking Innateness: A Connectionist Perspective on Development.* Cambridge, MA: Bradford Books and MIT Press.

Evans, N. and Levinson, S. (2009). The myth of language universals: Language diversity and its importance for cognitive science. *Behavioral and Brain Sciences* 32, 429–448.

Fillmore, C. J. (1968). The case for case. In E. Bach and R. T. Harms (eds.), *Universals in Linguistic Theory*, 1–81. New York: Holt, Reinhart & Winston.

Fillmore, C. J. (1982). Frame semantics. In D. Geeraerts (ed.), *Cognitive Linguistics. Basic Readings*, 373–400. Berlin: Mouton de Gruyter.

Fillmore, C. J. and Kay, P. (1999). *Construction Grammar*. Berkeley: University of California. Unpublished manuscript.

Fillmore, C. J., Kay, P., and O'Connor, C. (1988). Regularity and idiomaticity in grammatical constructions: The case of *let alone*. *Language* 64, 501–538.

Fonteyn, L. and Van de Pol, N. (2016). Divide and conquer: The formation and functional dynamics of the Modern English *ing*-clause network. *English Language and Linguistics* 20, 185–219.

Gahl, S. and Garnsey, S. M. (2004). Knowledge of grammar, knowledge of usage: Syntactic probabilities affect pronunciation variation. *Language* 80, 748–775.

Gahl, S., Yao, Y., and Johnson, K. (2012). Why reduce? Phonological neighborhood density and phonetic reduction in spontaneous speech. *Journal of Memory and Language* 66, 789–806.

Garnsey, S. M., Pearlmutter, N. J., Myers, E. M., and Lotocky, M. A. (1997). The contributions of verb bias and plausibility to the comprehension of temporarily ambiguous sentences. *Journal of Memory and Language* 7, 58–93.

Gentner, D. (1983). Structure-mapping: A theoretical framework for analogy. *Cognitive Science* 7, 155–170.

Goldberg, A. E. (1995). *Constructions: A Construction Grammar Approach to Argument Structure*. Chicago, IL: University of Chicago Press.

Goldberg, A. E. (2003). Constructions: A new theoretical approach to language. *Trends in Cognitive Sciences* 7, 219–224.

Goldberg, A. E. (2006). *Constructions at Work: The Nature of Generalization in Language*. Oxford: Oxford University Press.

Goldberg, A. E. (2019). *Explain Me This: Creativity, Competition, and the Partial Productivity of Constructions*. Princeton, NJ: Princeton University Press.

Goldberg, A. E. and Jackendoff, R. S. (2004). The English resultative as a family of constructions. *Language* 80, 532–567.

Greenberg, J. H. (1966). *Language Universals, with Special Reference to Feature Hierarchies*. The Hague: Mouton.

Grice, H. P. (1975). Logic and Conversation. In P. Cole and J. Morgan (eds.), *Syntax and Semantics*, Vol. 3, 41–58. New York: Academic Press.

Gries, S. T. (2003). *Multifactorial Analysis in Corpus Linguistics: A Study of Particle Placement*. London: Continuum.

Gries, S. T. (2005). Syntactic priming: A corpus-based approach. *Journal of Psycholinguistic Research* 34, 365–399.

Gries, S. T. and Stefanowitsch, A. (2004). Extending collexeme analysis. *International Journal of Corpus Linguistics* 9, 97–129.

Gries, S. T., Hampe, B., and Schönefeld, D. (2005). Converging evidence: Bringing together experimental and corpus data on the association of verbs and constructions. *Cognitive Linguistics* 16, 635–676.

Haig, G. (1998). *Relative Constructions in Turkish*. Wiesbaden: Harrassowitz.

Hare, M. L. and Goldberg, A. E. (2000). Structural priming: Purely syntactic? In M. Hahn and S. C. Stoness (eds.), *Proceedings of the 21st Annual Meeting of the Cognitive Science Society*, 208–211. New York: Psychology Press.

Hartmann, S. and Pleyer, M. (2020). Constructing a protolanguage: Reconstructing prehistoric languages in a usage-based construction grammar framework. *Philosophical Transactions of the Royal Society* B 376, 20200200.

Haspelmath, M. (2021). Explaining grammatical coding asymmetries: Form–frequency correspondences and predictability. *Journal of Linguistics* 57, 605–633.

Haspelmath, M., Calude, A., Spagnol, M., Narrog, H., and Bamyaci, E. (2014). Coding causal-noncausal verb alternations: A form-frequency correspondence explanation. *Journal of Linguistics* 50, 587–625.

Haspelmath, M. and Karjus, A. (2017). Explaining asymmetries in number marking: Singulatives, pluratives, and usage frequency. *Linguistics* 55, 1213–1235.

Hawkins, J. A. (2004). *Efficiency and Complexity in Grammars*. Oxford: Oxford University Press.

Heine, B., Claudi, U., and Hünnemeyer, F. (1991). *Grammaticalization. A Conceptual Framework*. Chicago, IL: Chicago University Press.

Herbst, T. (2014). The valency approach to argument structure constructions. In T. Herbst, H.-J. Schmid, and S. Faulhaber (eds.), *Constructions – Collocations – Patterns*, 167–216. Berlin: Mouton de Gruyter.

Hetterle, K. (2015). *Adverbial Clauses in Cross-Linguistic Perspective*. Berlin: Mouton de Gruyter.

Hilpert, M. (2013). *Constructional Change in English: Developments in Allomorphy, Word-Formation and Syntax*. Cambridge: Cambridge University Press.

Hilpert, M. (2014). *Construction Grammar and Its Application to English*. Edinburgh: Edinburgh University Press.

Hilpert, M. (2021). *Ten Lectures on Diachronic Construction Grammar*. Leiden: Brill.

Hilpert, M. and Flach, S. (2022). A case of constructional contamination in English: Modified noun phrases influence adverb placement in the passive. In K. Krawczak, B. Lewandowska-Tomaszczyk, and M. Grygiel (eds.), *Contrast and Analogy in Language: Perspectives from Cognitive Linguistics*. Amsterdam: John Benjamins.

Höder, S. (2012). Multilingual constructions. In K. Braunmüller and C. Gabriel (eds.), *Multilingual Individuals and Multilingual Societies*, 241–258. Amsterdam: John Benjamins.

Hoffmann, T. (2011). *Particle Placement in English: A Usage-based Approach*. Cambridge: Cambridge University Press.

Hoffmann, T. (2019). *English Comparative Correlatives: Diachronic and Synchronic Variation at the Lexicon-Syntax Interface*. Cambridge: Cambridge University Press.

Hoffmann, T. (2020). What would it take for us to abandon construction Grammar? Falsifiability, confirmation bias and the future of the constructionist enterprise. *Belgian Journal of Linguistics* 34, 149–161.

Hoffmann, T. (2022). *Construction Grammar: The Structure of English*. Cambridge: Cambridge University Press.

Hoffmann, T. and Trousdale, G. (eds.), (2013). *The Oxford Handbook of Construction Grammar*. Oxford: Oxford University Press.

Hopper, P. J. (1987). Emergent grammar. *Berkeley Linguistics Society* 13, 139–157.

Hopper, P. J. and Thompson, S. A. (1984). The discourse basis for lexical categories in universal grammar. *Language* 60, 703–752.

Huddleston, R. and Pullum, G. (2002). *The Cambridge Grammar of the English language*. Cambridge: Cambridge University Press.

Hudson, R. (2007). *Language Networks. The New Word Grammar*. Oxford: Oxford University Press.

Ibbotson, P. (2020). *What It Takes to Talk: Exploring Developmental Cognitive Linguistics*. Berlin: Mouton de Gruyter.

Israel, M. (1996). The *way* constructions grow. In A. E. Goldberg (ed.), *Conceptual Structure, Discourse and Language*, 217–230. Stanford: CSLI.

Iwasaki, S. (2013). *Japanese*. Amsterdam: John Benjamins.

Iwata, S. (2008). *Locative Alternation: A Lexicalist-Constructional Approach*. Amsterdam: John Benjamins.

Jackendoff, R. (1997). Twistin' the night away. *Language* 73, 534–559.

Jackendoff, R. (2002a). *Foundations of Language: Brain, Meaning, Grammar, Evolution*. Oxford: Oxford University Press.

Jackendoff, R. (2002b). English particle constructions, the lexicon, and the autonomy of syntax. In N. Dehé, R. Jackendoff, A. McIntyre, and S. Urban (eds.), *Verb-Particle Explorations*, 67–94. Berlin: Mouton de Gruyter.

Jackendoff, R. and Audring, J. (2020). *The Texture of the Lexicon: Relational Morphology and the Parallel Architecture*. Oxford: Oxford University Press.

Janda, L. A. (2013). *Cognitive Linguistics: The Quantitative Turn*. Berlin: Mouton de Gruyter.

Jurafsky, D. (1991). An on-line computational model of human sentence interpretation: A theory of the representation and use of linguistic knowledge. PhD dissertation. University of California, Berkeley.

Jurafsky, D. (1996). A probabilistic model of lexical and syntactic access and disambiguation. *Cognitive Science* 20, 137–194.

Justeson, J. S. and Stephens, L. D. (1990). Explanations for word order universals: A log-linear analysis. In W. Bahner, J. Schildt, and D. Viehweger (eds.), *Proceedings of the XIV International Congress of Linguistics*, Vol. 3, 2372–2376. Berlin: Mouton de Gruyter.

Kamide, Y., Altmann, G. T. M., and Haywood, S. L. (2003). The time-course of prediction in incremental sentence processing: Evidence from anticipatory eye movements. *Journal of Memory and Language* 49, 133–156.

Kapatsinski, V. (2018). *Changing Minds, Changing Tools: From Learning Theory to Language Acquisition to Language Change*. Cambridge, MA: MIT Press.

König, E. and Siemund, P. (2007). Speech act distinctions in grammar. In T. Shopen (ed.), *Language Typology and Syntactic Description, Vol. 1: Clause Structure*, 276–324. Cambridge: Cambridge University Press.

Krug, M. (2000). *Emerging English Modals: A Corpus-based Study of Grammaticalization*. Berlin: Mouton de Gruyter.

Kuperberg, G. R. and Jaeger, T. F. (2016). What do we mean by prediction in language comprehension. *Language, Cognition and Neuroscience* 31, 32–59.

Lakoff, G. (1987). *Women, Fire, and Dangerous Things*. Chicago, IL: Chicago University Press.

Langacker, R. W. (1987). *Foundations of Cognitive Grammar, Vol. 1: Theoretical Prerequisites*. Stanford, CA: Stanford University Press.

Langacker, R. W. (1991). *Concept, Image, and Symbol: The Cognitive Basis of Grammar*. Berlin: Mouton de Gruyter.

Langacker, R. W. (1997). Constituency, dependency, and conceptual grouping. *Cognitive Linguistics* 8, 1–32.

Langacker, R. W. (2000). A dynamic usage-based model. In S. Kemmer and M. Barlow (eds.), *Usage-Based Models of Language*, 1–64. Stanford, CA: Center for the Study of Language and Information (CSLI).

Langacker, R. W. (2008). *Cognitive Grammar: A Basic Introduction*. Oxford: Oxford University Press.

Lasch, A. and Ziem, A. (eds.), (2014). *Grammatik als Netzwerk von Konstruktionen: Sprachwissen im Fokus der Konstruktionsgrammatik*. Berlin: Mouton de Gruyter.

Leino, J. (2021). Formalizing paradigms in construction grammar. In G. Diewald and K. Politt (eds.), *Paradigms Regained: Theoretical and Empirical Arguments for the Assessment of the Notion of Paradigm*, 37–66. Leipzig: Language Science Press.

Levshina, N. (2022). *Communicative Efficiency: Language Structure and Use*. Cambridge: Cambridge University Press.

Lieven, E. V. M., Behrens, H., Spears, J., and Tomasello, M. (2003). Early syntactic creativity: A usage-based approach. *Journal of Child Language* 30, 333–370.

Logan, G. D. (1988). Towards an instance theory of automatization. *Psychological Review* 95, 492–527.

Lorenz, D. (2020). Converging variations and the emergence of horizontal links: *To*-contraction in American English. In L. Sommerer and E. Smirnova. (eds.), *Nodes and Networks in Diachronic Construction Grammar*, 243–276. Amsterdam: John Benjamins.

Lorenz, D. and Tizón-Couto, D. (2020). Not just frequency, not just modality: Production and perception of English semi-modals. In P. Hohaus and R. Schulze (eds.), *Re-Assessing Modalising Expressions: Categories, Co-text, and Context*, 79-108. Amsterdam: John Benjamins.

Luce, P. A. and Pisoni, D. P. (1998). Recognizing spoken words: The neighborhood activation model. *Ear and Hearing* 19, 1–36.

Lyngfelt, B. (2018). Introduction: Constructions and constructicography. In B. Lyngfelt, L. Borin, K. H. Ohara, and T. T. Torrent (eds.), *Constructicography: Constructicon Development across Languages*, 1–18. Amsterdam: John Benjamins.

Lyngfelt, B., Borin, L., Ohara, K. H., and Torrent, T. T. (eds.), (2018). *Constructicography: Constructicon Development across Languages*. Amsterdam: John Benjamins.

MacDonald, M. C., Pearlmutter, N. J., and Seidenberg, M. S. (1994). Lexical nature of syntactic ambiguity resolution. *Psychological Review* 101, 676–703.

MacDonald, M. C. and Seidenberg, M. S. (2006). Constraint satisfaction accounts of lexical and sentence comprehension. In M. J. Traxlor and M. A. Gernsbacher (eds.), *Handbook of Psycholinguistics*, 581–611. London: Elsevier.

Malchukov, A. (1995). *Even*. Munich: Lincom Europe.

Manning, C. D. and Schütze, H. (1999). *Foundations of Statistical Natural Language Processing*. Cambridge, MA: MIT Press.

Maye, J., Werker, J. F., and Gerken, L. (2002). Infant sensitivity to distributional information can affect phonetic discrimination. *Cognition* 82, B101–B111.

Michaelis, L. A. (2013). Sign-based construction grammar. In T. Hoffmann and G. Trousdale (eds.), *The Oxford Handbook of Construction Grammar*, 133–152. Oxford: Oxford University Press.

Michaelis, L. A. and Lambrecht, K. (1996). Toward a construction-based theory of language function: The case of nominal extraposition. *Language* 72, 215–247.

Miestamo, M. (2005). *Standard Negation: The Negation of Declarative Verbal Main Clauses in a Typological Perspective*. Berlin: Mouton de Gruyter.

Norde, M. and Morris, C. (2018). Derivation without category change: A network-based analysis of diminutive prefixoids in Dutch. In K. Van Goethem, M. Norde, E. Coussé, and G. Vanderbauwhede (eds.), *Category Change from a Constructional Perspective*, 47–92. Amsterdam: John Benjamins.

Nosofsky, R. M. (1988). Similarity, frequency and category representation. *Journal of Experimental Psychology: Learning, Memory and Cognition* 14, 54–65.

Nunberg, G., Sag, I. A., and Wasow, T. (1994). Idioms. *Language* 70, 491–538.

Perek, F. (2015). *Argument Structure in Usage-Based Construction Grammar: Experimental and Corpus-Based Perspectives*. Amsterdam: John Benjamins.

Perek, F. and Goldberg, A. E. (2015). Generalizing beyond the input: The functions of the constructions matter. *Journal of Memory and Language* 24, 108–127.

Petré, P. (2014). *Constructions and Environments: Copular, Passive, and Related Constructions in Old and Middle English*. Oxford: Oxford University Press.

Pickering, M. J. and Branigan, H. P. (1998). The representation of verbs: Evidence from syntactic priming in language production. *Journal of Memory and Language* 39, 633–651.

Pickering, M. J. and Ferreira, V. S. (2008). Structural priming. A critical review. *Psychological Bulletin* 134, 427–459.

Pierrehumbert, J. B. (2003). Phonetic diversity, statistical learning, and the acquisition of phonology. *Language and Speech* 46, 115–154

Pijpops, D., De Smet, I., and Van de Velde, F. (2018). Constructional contamination in morphology and syntax. *Constructions and Frames* 10, 269–305.

Pijpops, D. and Van de Velde, F. (2016). Constructional contamination: How does it work and how do we measure it? *Folia Linguistica* 50, 543–581.

Pinker, S. (1989). *Learnability and Cognition: The Acquisition of Argument Structure*. Cambridge, MA: MIT Press.

Sag, I. A. (2012). Sign-based construction grammar. In H. C. Boas and I. A. Sag (eds.), *Sign-Based Construction Grammar*, 69–202. Stanford, CA: Center for the Study of Language and Information (CSLI).

Sapir, E. (1921). *Language: An Introduction to the Study of Speech*. New York: Harcourt Brace Jovanovich.

Schmid, H.-J. (2016). A framework for understanding entrenchment and its psychological foundations. In H. J. Schmid (ed.), *Entrenchment and the Psychology of Language Learning*, 9–39. Berlin: Mouton de Gruyter.

Schmid, H.-J. (2020). *The Dynamics of the Linguistic System: Usage, Conventionalization and Entrenchment*. Oxford: Oxford University Press.

Schmidtke-Bode, K. and Diessel, H. (2017). Cross-linguistic patterns in the structure, function and position of (object) complement clauses. *Linguistics* 55, 1–38.

Schmidtke-Bode, K. and Levshina, N. (2018). Reassessing scale effects on differential object marking: Methodological, conceptual and theoretical issues in quest of a universal. In I. A. Seržant and A. Witzlack-Makarevich (eds.), *Diachrony of Differential Object Marking*, 509–538. Leipzig: Language Science Press.

Schreuder, R. and Baayen, H. R. (1997). How complex simplex words can be. *Journal of Memory and Language* 37, 118–139.

Searle, J. R. (1969). *Speech Acts*. Cambridge: Cambridge University Press.

Shieber, S. (2003). *An Introduction to Unification-Based Approaches to Grammar*. Brookline, MA: Microtome Publishing. [first published 1986]

Smirnova, E. (2021). Horizontal links within and between paradigms. In M. Hilpert, B. Cappelle, and I. Depraetere (eds.), *Modality and Diachronic Construction Grammar*, 185–218. Amsterdam: John Benjamins.

Sommerer, L. (2018). *Article Emergence in Old English: A Constructionalist Perspective*. Berlin: Mouton de Gruyter.

Sommerer, L. (2022). Day to day and night after night: Temporal NPN constructions in Present Day English. In L. Sommerer and E. Keizer (eds.), *English Noun Phrases from a Functional-Cognitive Perspective*, 363–394. Amsterdam: John Benjamins.

Sommerer, L. and Smirnova, E. (eds.), (2020). *Nodes and Networks in Diachronic Construction Grammar*. Amsterdam: John Benjamins.

Sporns, O. (2012). *Networks of the Brain*. Cambridge, MA: MIT Press.

Steels, L. (2011), (ed.). *Design Patterns of Fluid Construction Grammar*. Berlin: Mouton de Gruyter.

Steels, L. (2015). *The Talking Heads Experiment: Origins of Words and Meanings*. Berlin: Language Science Press.

Stefanowitsch, A. and Gries, S. (2003). Collostructions: Investigating the interaction of words and constructions. *International Journal of Corpus Linguistics* 8, 209–243.

Tomasello, M. (2003). *Constructing a Language: A Usage-Based Approach.* Cambridge, MA: Harvard University Press.

Traugott, E. C. and Trousdale, G. (2013). *Constructionalization and Constructional Changes.* Oxford: Oxford University Press.

Trueswell, J. C. (1996). The role of lexical frequency in syntactic ambiguity resolution. *Journal of Memory and Language* 35, 566–585.

Ungerer, T. (2021). Using structural priming to test links between constructions: English caused-motion and resultative sentences inhibit each other. *Cognitive Linguistics* 32, 389–420.

Ungerer, T. and Hartmann, S. (2023). *Constructionist Approaches: Past, Present, Future.* Cambridge: Cambridge University Press.

Van de Velde, F. (2010). The emergence of the determiner in Dutch NP. *Linguistics* 48, 263–299.

Van de Velde, F. (2014). Degeneracy: The maintenance of constructional networks. In R. Boogaart, T. Colleman, and G. Rutten (eds.), *Extending the Scope of Construction Grammar*, 141–179. Berlin: Mouton de Gruyter.

van Lier, E. and Messerschmidt, M. (2022). Lexical restrictions on grammatical relations in voice and valency constructions. *STUF – Language Typology and Universals* 75, 1–20.

Van Trijp, R. (2016). *The Evolution of Case Grammar.* Leipzig: Language Science Press.

Vitevitch, M. S. (2002). The influence of phonological neighbourhoods on speech production. *Journal of Experimental Psychology*: *Learning, Memory and Cognition* 28, 735–747.

Wells, J. B., Christiansen, M. H., Race, D. S., Acheson, D. J., and MacDonald, M. C. (2009). Experience and sentence processing: Statistical learning and relative clause comprehension. *Cognitive Psychology* 58, 250–271.

Werker, J. F., Yeung, H. H., and Yoshhida, K. A. (2012). How do infants become experts of native-speech pronunciation? *Current Directions in Psychological Science* 21, 221–226.

Wiechmann, D. (2008). Sense-contingent lexical preferences and early parsing decisions: Corpus-evidence from local NP/S-ambiguities. *Cognitive Linguistics* 19, 447–463.

Willich, A. (2022). *Konstruktionssemantik: Frames in gebrauchsbasierter Konstruktions-grammatik und Konstruktikographie.* Berlin: Mouton de Gruyter.

Wolk, C., Bresnan, J., Rosenbach, A., and Szmrecsanyi, B. (2013). Dative and genitive variability in Late Modern English: Exploring cross-constructional variation and change. *Diachronica* 30, 382–419.

Zehnenter, E. (2019). *Competition in Language Change: The Rise and Fall of the English Dative Alternation*. Berlin: Mouton de Gruyter.

Construction Grammar

Thomas Hoffmann

Catholic University of Eichstätt-Ingolstadt

Thomas Hoffmann is Full Professor and Chair of English Language and Linguistics at the Catholic University of Eichstätt-Ingolstadt as well as Furong Scholar Distinguished Chair Professor of Hunan Normal University. His main research interests are usage-based Construction Grammar, language variation and change and linguistic creativity. He has published widely in international journals such as *Cognitive Linguistics, English Language and Linguistics,* and *English World-Wide.* His monographs *Preposition Placement in English* (2011) and *English Comparative Correlatives: Diachronic and Synchronic Variation at the Lexicon-Syntax Interface* (2019) were both published by Cambridge University Press. His textbook on *Construction Grammar: The Structure of English* (2022) as well as an Element on *The Cognitive Foundation of Post-colonial Englishes: Construction Grammar as the Cognitive Theory for the Dynamic Model* (2021) have also both been published with Cambridge University Press. He is also co-editor (with Graeme Trousdale) of *The Oxford Handbook of Construction Grammar* (2013, Oxford University Press).

Alexander Bergs

Osnabrück University

Alexander Bergs joined the Institute for English and American Studies at Osnabrück University, Germany, in 2006 when he became Full Professor and Chair of English Language and Linguistics. His research interests include, among others, language variation and change, constructional approaches to language, the role of context in language, the syntax/ pragmatics interface, and cognitive poetics. His works include several authored and edited books (*Social Networks and Historical Sociolinguistics, Modern Scots, Contexts and Constructions, Constructions and Language Change*), a short textbook on *Synchronic English Linguistics,* one on *Understanding Language Change* (with Kate Burridge) and the two-volume *Handbook of English Historical Linguistics* (ed. with Laurel Brinton; now available as five-volume paperback) as well as more than fifty papers in high-profile international journals and edited volumes. Alexander Bergs has taught at the Universities of Düsseldorf, Bonn, Santiago de Compostela, Wisconsin-Milwaukee, Catania, Vigo, Thessaloniki, Athens, and Dalian and has organized numerous international workshops and conferences.

About the Series

Construction Grammar is the leading cognitive theory of syntax. The present Elements series will survey its theoretical building blocks, show how Construction Grammar can capture various linguistic phenomena across a wide range of typologically different languages, and identify emerging frontier topics from a theoretical, empirical and applied perspective.

Cambridge Elements $\equiv$

Construction Grammar

Elements in the Series

The Constructicon: Taxonomies and Networks
Holger Diessel

A full series listing is available at: www.cambridge.org/EICG

Printed in the United States
by Baker & Taylor Publisher Services